AROUND IPSWICH BY TROLLEYBUS

COLIN BARKER

Published by Adam Gordon

With the Lloyds building and archway providing the backdrop for this photograph, Ransomes 38 waits at the Cornhill stand from Princes Street before departing to Adair Road on Service 8 in August 1950. 38 was delivered in 1928, and withdrawn in 1953, giving just under 25 years' service. Originally, the front was to a half cab design to allow for "one man pay as you enter", but subsequently modified with a full front and entrance closed off as seen in this immediate post war view.
(C. Carter)

Front Cover. Incoming Sunbeam 116 turns out of Crown Street into Tower Street, the latter forming the eastern side of the Electric House terminus. A Morris Minor convertible is parked in Neale Street on the left.
(A. Belton)

Rear Cover. Sunbeam 117 waits before leaving the Rushmere Heath terminus of Service 3 to re-join Woodbridge Road East, and then cross town to Whitton as Service 9. The split Gordon's gin advertisement each side of the destination frequently appeared on Ipswich vehicles.
(A. Belton)

Copyright – All rights reserved. No part of this publication may be reproduced, stored in a retrieval system or transmitted in any form or by any means, electronic, mechanical, photocopying, recording or otherwise without the prior permission in writing from the publishers.

ISBN 978-1-910654-33-0

Publication no. 137

Published in 2022 by Adam Gordon, Kintradwell Farmhouse, Brora, Sutherland, KW9 6LU
Tel: 01408 622660 E-mail: adam@ahg-books.com

Designed and typeset by Barnabas Gordon
Tel: 07795 201 502 Email: Barney@ahgbooks.com

Printed by Henry Ling Ltd., The Dorset Press, Dorchester, DT1 1HD

CONTENTS

INTRODUCTION	4
ACKNOWLEDGEMENTS	5
WIRING MAPS	6
A STEP BACK IN TIME	8
SERVICES 1/1A - BOURNE BRIDGE/TYLER STREET	10
SERVICES 2/2A - PRIORY HEATH/ AIRPORT	12
SERVICES 3/3A & 9/9A - RUSHMERE HEATH/ LATTICE BARN	37
SERVICE 4 - ST AUGUSTINE'S/KINGS WAY FOR DEPOT WORKINGS	56
SERVICE 5 - FOXHALL ROAD	74
SERVICE 6/6A/6B - GAINSBOROUGH CIRCULARS	80
SERVICES 7/7A - CHANTRY PARK/HADLEIGH ROAD	105
SERVICES 8/8A - ADAIR ROAD/BRAMFORD ROAD BRIDGE	108
SERVICE X - STATION	115
SERVICE 11 - SIDEGATE LANE	125
SERVICE 0/- - CIRCULARS/COLCHESTER ROAD	131
DEPOTS	137
THE AFTER LIFE	145
THE END OF AN ERA	152
FLEET LIST	155

INTRODUCTION

This is the second book in this series that I have completed, the first being on the trolleybuses of my home town of Derby, where my childhood interest in these vehicles began in the early 1940s. This second publication covers the trolleybuses of my adopted town of Ipswich, having moved to Suffolk with my employment in 1991.

My only experience of the Ipswich system was as a result of a works trip to Stowmarket and Felixstowe in the mid 1950s when I was an apprentice. As we passed the outer fringes of the town, in the distance I caught sight of a trolleybus parked on the Priory Heath depot forecourt.

The town was unusual in only operating trolleybuses until the first motorbuses arrived in 1950, and prior to the nationalisation of the electricity industry in the late 1940s, the town's electricity supply and transport departments were operated as a single entity.

When the decision was made to replace trams with trolleybuses in 1925, the town officials supported local Suffolk industry in placing initial bulk orders with Garretts of Leiston and Ransomes Sims and Jefferies of Ipswich. The latter company continued to supply chassis to the undertaking up to the outbreak of the Second World War.

Ipswich is the county town of Suffolk, historically serving the vast agricultural areas beyond. The town lies on the River Orwell with access to the North Sea, which led to the early development of the dock area and shipbuilding. The growth of industry resulted in the major re-development of the docks, thereby creating a thriving eastern port. With the gradual increase in craft size, the major dock area has moved further down river, with the older central facility now mainly devoted to leisure craft.

After the First World War, the electric tramway system was in poor shape and, although some track was renewed, thoughts turned towards the use of trolleybuses. A pilot project was introduced with three single deck vehicles hired from Railless Limited, running from the Cornhill to Ipswich railway station. The service commenced on 2nd September 1923, and its success led the Corporation to obtain an Act of Parliament to replace the trams with trolleybuses following a local referendum of ratepayers, resulting in a minority wanting motorbuses to be the replacing vehicles. Service conversions quickly followed, with the last tram being withdrawn on 26th July 1926; six trams, plus one body, were sold to Scarborough Tramways.

Prior to 1934, the central hub of the trolleybus system was the Cornhill, but when services were provided for that year's Royal Agricultural Show, additional turning facilities were provided at Electric House to cope with the crowds wanting to attend. The name of the latter relates to an office building opened in 1932 for the Borough's Electricity Department; the Electric House destination name was used by trolleybuses from 1935.

The combination of new postwar housing estates, reduced numbers of chassis builders and overhead equipment suppliers, and the fact the Council could no longer control the electricity charges following the nationalisation of the electricity industry by the post war Labour Government, led to the decision to introduce the first motorbus service in May 1950. Some trolleybus services were withdrawn in 1951, and thereafter motorbuses began to replace trolleybuses, with the final closure of the system on 23rd August 1963. So ended 60 years of electric traction along Ipswich streets, with trolleybuses having contributed 40 years of service.

Whilst the content of this publication will be of interest to trolleybus enthusiasts, I have pitched the caption texts as though the reader was visiting Ipswich for the first time, and learning about the town and its suburbs by travelling around the system. Therefore, although the pictures depict trolleybuses in service, the captions also refer to the surrounding areas, pointing out how the town has changed over the last 70 years.

ACKNOWLEDGEMENTS

The photographs contained in this publication originate from a wide variety of sources including fellow enthusiasts, private collections and transport societies, with due accreditation given where known. Inevitably, some photographs give no indication of their origin, or current copyright holders. I hope they will accept that the photographer's work has been chosen so that their efforts can be appreciated by a wider audience.

Special thanks go to Stephen Lockwood, Hugh Taylor, Tony Belton, David Pearson and the Ipswich Transport Museum for giving me access to their extensive photographic collections, and Roger Smith for his excellent wiring maps. Additional thanks go to Tony for his sterling efforts in scanning Peter Mitchell's negatives. Brian Dyes and Stuart Ray of the Ipswich Transport Museum, who both answered my interminable questions, plus Hugh Taylor, read through the original draft, which resulted in many constructive suggestions. Beaulieu Motor Museum helped with a number of vehicle identifications. Finally, I must thank my wife, Maureen, for her support whilst compiling this publication, and using her computer skills in providing usable material for the publisher.

Although all the services are shown as departing from the Town Centre, (other than Services 3 and 9), many were linked over the years to provide cross town services; these links varied as the system grew. In most cases, on reaching the outer termini, the blind would be changed to show the eventual cross-town destination. Much of the redundant overhead wiring left after any service withdrawal was used by school and workmen's specials, plus depot access.

All post war deliveries were bodied by Park Royal; only bodybuilders other than this will be identified in the picture captions. All the pre-war single deck vehicles, and the first double deckers, had both the chassis and bodies built by Ransomes.

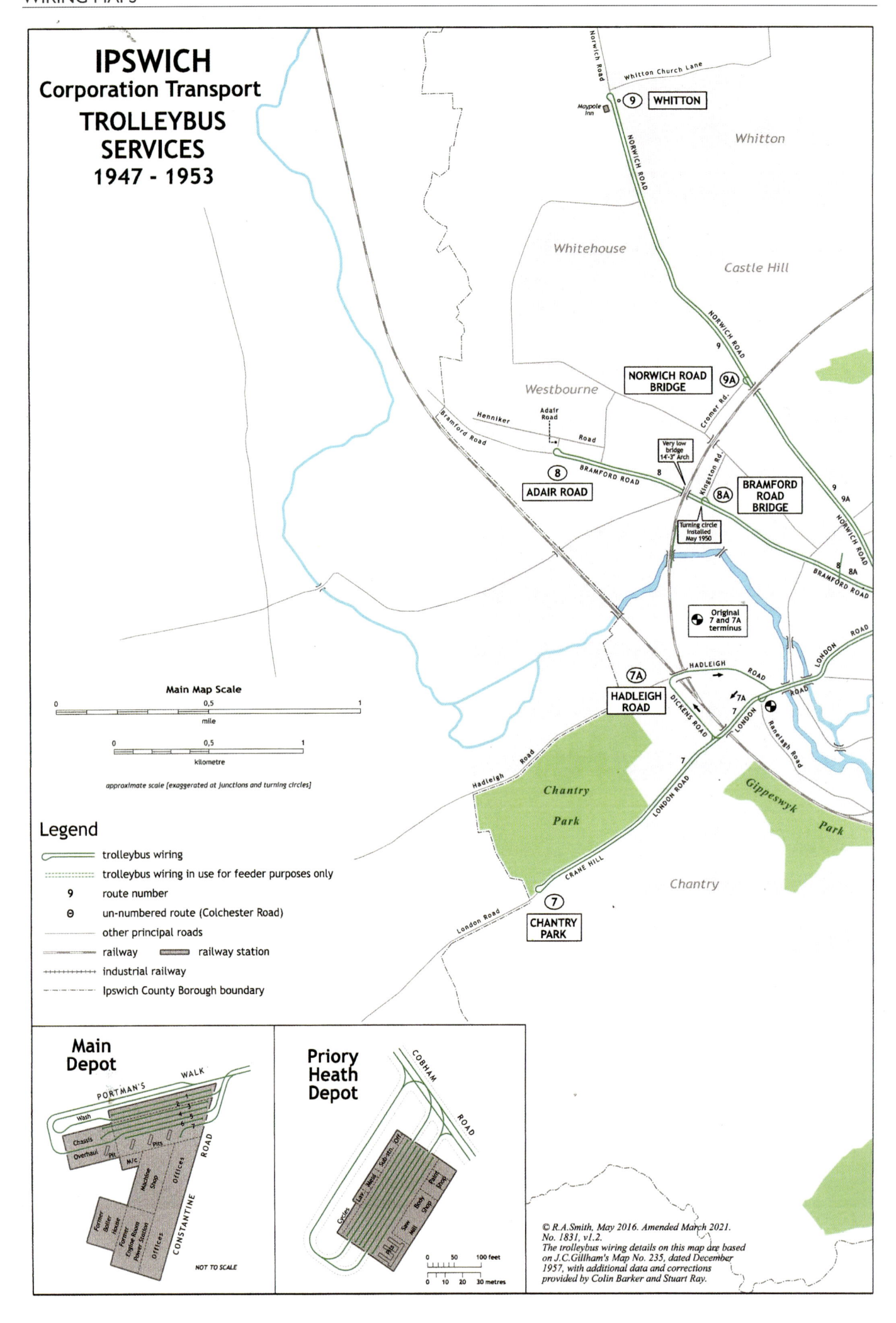

WIRING MAPS

IPSWICH Corporation Transport TROLLEYBUS SERVICES 1947 - 1953

Legend
- trolleybus wiring
- trolleybus wiring in use for feeder purposes only
- 9   route number
- ⊖   un-numbered route (Colchester Road)
- other principal roads
- railway   railway station
- industrial railway
- Ipswich County Borough boundary

Main Map Scale — 0 to 1 mile / 0 to 1 kilometre
approximate scale (exaggerated at junctions and turning circles)

Route points
- (9) WHITTON — Maypole Inn, Norwich Road / Whitton Church Lane
- (9A) NORWICH ROAD BRIDGE
- (8) ADAIR ROAD — Bramford Road
- (8A) BRAMFORD ROAD BRIDGE — Very low bridge 14'-3" Arch
- Turning circle installed May 1950
- Original 7 and 7A terminus
- (7A) HADLEIGH ROAD
- (7) CHANTRY PARK — London Road / Crane Hill

Areas shown: Whitton, Whitehouse, Castle Hill, Westbourne, Chantry Park, Gippeswyk Park, Chantry

Roads: Norwich Road, Cromer Rd., Bramford Road, Henniker Road, Adair Road, Kingston Rd., Hadleigh Road, Dickens Road, London Road, Ranelagh Road, Crane Hill

Main Depot
PORTMAN'S WALK, CONSTANTINE ROAD
- Wash, Chassis Overhaul, Pits, M/c, Machine Shop, Offices
- Former Boiler House, Former Engine Room Power Station, Offices
- Bays 1–7
NOT TO SCALE

Priory Heath Depot
COBHAM ROAD
- Cycles, Lav., Mess, Sub-stn., Offices, Body Shop, Paint Shop, Saw Mill
0–100 feet / 0–30 metres

© R.A.Smith, May 2016. Amended March 2021.
No. 1831, v1.2.
The trolleybus wiring details on this map are based on J.C.Gillham's Map No. 235, dated December 1957, with additional data and corrections provided by Colin Barker and Stuart Ray.

6

WIRING MAPS

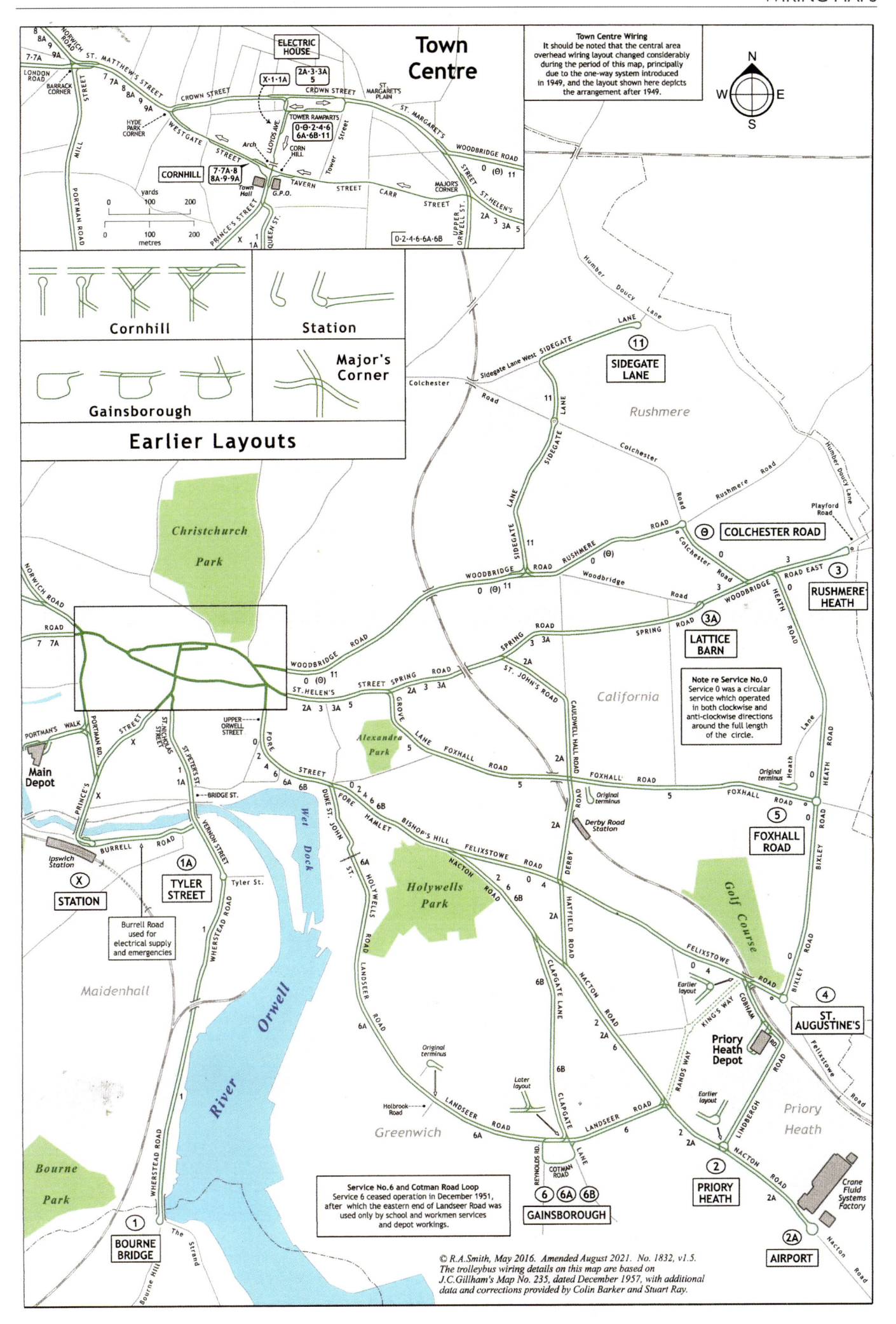

A STEP BACK IN TIME

Before looking at each of the Ipswich services, the following late 1920s images provide examples of the first deliveries of trolleybuses to replace the trams

In this Cornhill scene, one of the original Railless vehicles is about to leave Princes Street on the left, and make a 180 degree turn ready for the return journey to the Station. Tram track and overhead wiring continue along Westgate and Princes Streets. Traffic movement at the time appeared to warrant a policeman on point duty.
(Commercial postcard)

From this elevated position, the photographer has captured two vehicles in the Cornhill, with Tavern Street beyond. On the right is a Ransomes, possibly 12, waiting to turn into Princes Street and onward to Bourne Bridge on Service 1. On the left is Railless 2 with its open rear balcony. Horse drawn carriages for hire have now been replaced by motorised taxis. The person bottom centre appears to be holding a bamboo boom retrieval pole.
(Commercial postcard)

This picture shows the Cornhill looking towards Tavern Street, with the imposing Post Office building on the right. Beyond the statue recognising those killed in the Boer War, is one of three original vehicles supplied by Railless, which is about to complete the turn back into Princes Street on the right, and then onwards to the Station; this was the initial trial service before deciding on the conversion programme. Note the open rear platform for smokers, and the early railway carriage clerestory style roof. Immediately behind is a Garrett, one of fifteen delivered for the conversion, with a similar vehicle about to leave Tavern Street. Facing in the opposite direction is a Ransomes, also one of fifteen, which together with the Garretts initiated the tram to trolleybus conversion.
(Commercial postcard)

SERVICES 1/1A

1 TOWN CENTRE – VERNON STREET – WHERSTEAD ROAD - BOURNE BRIDGE
1A TOWN CENTRE – VERNON STREET - TYLER STREET (SHORT WORKING)

17/7/25	Tram service replaced by trolleybus using new concrete bridge over the River Orwell. Departure/return Cornhill.
8/8/33	Short working at junction with Tyler Street **(Service 1A)**.
??/7/49	Some town centre departures moved to Electric House (Lloyds Avenue).
22/5/54	Last day. Replaced by motorbus.

Sunbeam 120 passes over railway track in Bridge Street at the entrance to St Peter's Dock on the right in July 1952. The track was used by steam tram engines to move wagons between the dock area and marshalling sidings on the left, the latter now the site of a car park and retail outlets. The tower of St Peter's church is in the background.

(J. H. Meredith/Online Transport Archive)

At the Bourne Bridge terminus of Service 1 in July 1949, Ransomes 44 is about to begin the turn back to the town centre along Wherstead Road, and then onwards to Adair Road on Service 8. Full use is being made of the advertising boards; also note the large lifeguard between the front and rear wheels due to the high floor level.
(A. Gordon collection)

The driver of Ransomes 20 has engaged full lock to begin the tight Bourne Bridge turn and, having negotiated this, will also travel to Adair Road on Service 8. In the background the unique Massey bodied Ransome 86, delivered in 1940, is engaged on an enthusiasts' special.
(A. Gordon collection)

SERVICES 2/2A

2 TOWN CENTRE – NACTON ROAD – PRIORY HEATH
2A TOWN CENTRE – ST JOHN'S ROAD – NACTON ROAD – PRIORY HEATH – AIRPORT

Service 2 which became 2A

9/6/26	Tram service replaced by trolleybus. Service operated along St Helen's Street, and then along Spring, St John's and Cauldwell Hall Roads to Derby Road Station. Departure/return Cornhill.
18/3/28	Extended along Derby, Hatfield and Nacton Roads, then along Rands Way and Kings Way to join existing wiring on Felixstowe Road. Returned to the town centre via Felixstowe Road, Bishops Hill as **Service 4**, then retraced the route above. Destination display Rands Circle although no turning facility at this location.
6/12/36	Now terminated at Kings Way.
23/4/39	Extended along Nacton Road to Lindbergh Road (Priory Heath). Return to town centre as **Service 4** reintroduced (see above).
1939/40	Rands Way/Kings Way wiring no longer used. Retained for electrical supply purposes until 1951.
?/7/47	Departure moved to Electric House. Renumbered **Service 2A**.
17/8/47	Link with **Service 4** ceased. Now extended along Nacton Road to the Airport.
21/8/49	Inward to Cornhill. Then to Electric House via Westgate Street, Hyde Park Corner and Crown Street. Previously turned at the Station.
14/8/55	Most services replaced by motorbus.
28/7/56	Last day. Replaced by motorbus.

Service 2 introduced post 1936

??/??/??	Service opened to Kings Way via Bishops Hill and Nacton Road. Return to the town centre via Felixstowe Road, Bishops Hill as **Service 4**, then retrace the route above. Departure/return Electric House.
9/12/51	Now terminated at Priory Heath. Some services worked through to the Airport.
23/8/63	Last day. Replaced by motorbus.

Because of the intermingling of the two services, the photographic sequence for each has not been shown as separate sections

SERVICES 2/2A

Karrier W 101 waits under nearside overhead wiring on the south side of the Electric House terminal loop, before departing to the Airport, depicting Service 2 via Nacton Road. In later years some of Service 2 duties were extended beyond the normal Priory Heath terminus (Lindbergh Road) to the Airport. The department's duty office was immediately under the Wills's Woodbines advertisement.
(Author's collection)

This night time photograph depicts Sunbeam 116, and a sister vehicle behind, at Electric House with the former destined for the Airport as Service 2.
(A. Valentine/Ipswich Transport Museum)

The last day of trolleybus operation. Karrier 114 is seen leaving Electric House for the last time, with a more than full load, to return to the Priory Heath depot on the evening of 23rd August 1963. Suitably endorsed with RIP and bunting, it ended 40 years of trolleybus operation on the streets of Ipswich. Not the end for some vehicles however, as eight Sunbeams had already been sold to Walsall Corporation in 1962.
(G. R. Mortimer)

Having completed their shopping, the ladies take advantage of the seats under the shelter backing onto the Tower Ramparts School on the south side of the Electric House town centre terminus. Sunbeam 123 waits on stand before leaving for Priory Heath.
(Author's collection)

An immaculate Karrier W 107 has left the south side stand of the Electric House terminus, and sweeps round into Crown Street to make its way to Majors Corner, and onwards to Priory Heath. The three storey Egerton building dominates the background, with the car service reception entrance beyond the cyclists. The building has been replaced by the Crown Pools swimming and sports facility. The building on the far left has also disappeared.
(R. G. H. Simpson)

SERVICES 2/2A

Karrier 113 leaves Electric House for the Airport as Service 2 via Nacton Road; in the background is Karrier W 105 being used as a temporary crew canteen in 1963. 105 was withdrawn in 1962, and retained for use at a Civil Defence event later in the year, before its use as a canteen. It was purchased by the Ipswich Transport Museum, and painstakingly restored to working condition by the museum's volunteers. The culmination of all their hard work was to see 105 operating at the East Anglia Transport Museum, Carlton Colville, Lowestoft. The building on the extreme right is the corset factory of William Pretty and Sons, which was demolished in the 1980s to create a car park. (Photomatic Ltd)

15

SERVICES 2/2A

The driver of Ransomes 65 transfers booms between parallel wiring on the north side of the Electric House terminus. Note the side destination display. (R. Marshall/The Bus Archive)

Turning out of Crown Street into the short length of Tower Street, Karrier 113 makes its way to the Priory Heath stand on 14th October 1961. The overhead wiring leading in from the left was eventually removed as trolleybus services declined. The image on Page 58 illustrates this point. The Ford Popular on the left has a 1955 registration. (P. Mitchell)

On 16th June 1962, Karrier 111 approaches Tower Street from Crown Street on a return from Priory Heath, and will move to the stand for Service 2 on the north side of the Electric House terminus. In the background, wedding cars wait outside the Bethesda Baptist church. (P. Mitchell)

110 will shortly reach Electric House having just left St Margaret's Street, and is about to enter the short length of St Margaret's Plain which leads into Crown Street and the terminal wiring. Soane Street is off to the left beyond the zebra crossing. (A. Valentine/Ipswich Transport Museum)

SERVICES 2/2A

Karrier W 107 has just left St Margaret's Plain, and is about to enter the St Margaret's Street in May 1962. The destination is set for the Airport, but as an extension of Service 2 from Priory Heath. Traffic warranted a policeman on point duty at the junction with Great Colman Street on the left. Period cars, and a following Bedford lorry, complete the picture. (A. Gordon collection)

This view depicts the junction of St Margaret's Street with Woodbridge Road on the left, as Karrier 114 passes the policeman on point duty to continue along the former towards Majors Corner in June 1963. By the time this photograph was taken the overhead wiring along Woodbridge Road had been removed, as had the nearside wiring along St Margaret's Street towards Majors Corner. The area behind the advertising hoardings is the site of the second Odeon cinema building; the latter stood empty for nearly fifteen years before being purchased by the Hope Evangelical Church. (J. C. Gillham)

SERVICES 2/2A

On a cold winter's day, Karrier 112 moves along St Margaret's Street towards Electric House on a return trip from Priory Heath. Opposite is Soane Street, with an entrance to Christchurch Park on the left.
(A. Valentine/Ipswich Transport Museum)

Sunbeam 116 moves along St Margaret's Street past the junction with Woodbridge Road on the left, where wiring has been removed by the time this photograph was taken. A Hillman Minx passes in the opposite direction, beyond which is a washing powder advertisement mounted on the fencing surrounding the site of the second Odeon cinema.
(A. Valentine/Ipswich Transport Museum)

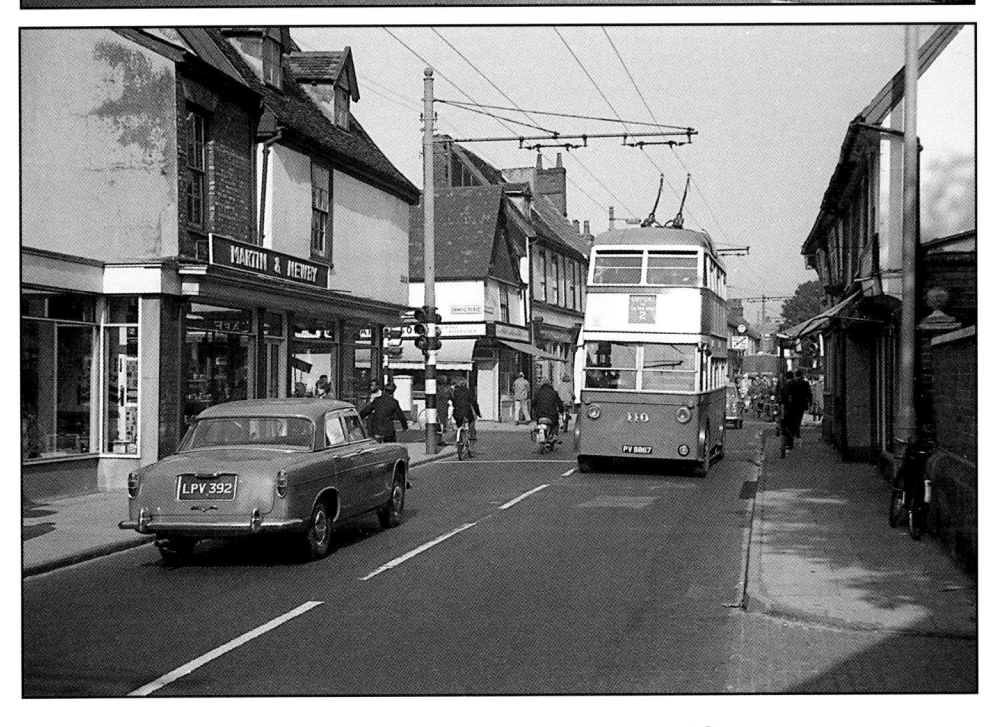

Karrier 110 leaves Upper Orwell Street, and enters Fore Street at the junction with Orwell Place on the left. A Rover P5 passes the long established premises of ironmongers Martin and Newby. (A. Valentine/Ipswich Transport Museum)

On a snowy day, and with the junction with Salthouse Street in the distance, the gentleman in the foreground appears keen for Karrier 111 to stop so he can board; 111 is destined for the Airport displaying Service 2. All the period buildings still exist, and in the foreground is a 1938 Austin Seven Ruby. (A. Valentine/Ipswich Transport Museum)

Having navigated the traffic island at the junction of Fore Street and Duke Street in the background, Karrier W 108 passes St Clements Congregational church to begin the climb up Fore Hamlet en route to Priory Heath. The church has now been converted into apartments.
(A. Valentine/Ipswich Transport Museum)

With the Gardeners Arms public house behind the Esso advertisement, Sunbeam 118 is about to exit Fore Hamlet before entering the steep climb up Bishops Hill. The glazed building behind 118 is now occupied by Enterprise Car Rentals, and the junction in front of the Esso sign leads into Cavendish Street. Today the lady on the scooter would be wearing a helmet.
(A. Valentine/Ipswich Transport Museum)

With the White Elm public house on the left, Karrier 114 descends Bishops Hill on 16th April 1955 on a return to the town centre. The parked Ford van belonged to A E L Tyler based in Felixstowe Road.
(P. Mitchell)

SERVICES 2/2A

On a wet day in June 1963, Karrier W 107 leaves the junction of Nacton Road, to the rear of the photographer, and Felixstowe Road as it prepares to drop down Bishops Hill to Fore Hamlet. A Standard 10 leads a number of period cars, with a Leicester registered unidentified pre-war vehicle about to follow 107.
(J. C. Gillham)

SERVICES 2/2A

On a snowy day, Karrier Ws 107 and 108 meet at the junction of Felixstowe and Nacton Roads. 107 is about to drop down Bishops Hill, and 108 has entered Nacton Road on Service 6B to Gainsborough.
(A. Valentine/Ipswich Transport Museum)

With the top of Bishops Hill in the distance, Sunbeam 115 begins the journey along an almost deserted Nacton Road displaying Service 2, but destined for the Airport.
(A. Valentine/Ipswich Transport Museum)

Almost at the same location, but looking in the opposite direction, Karriers 106 and 114 pass. Behind the wall on the right lies Holywells Park, which extends over 69 acres, and is a conservation area with two listed buildings, namely the stable block, and a conservatory.
(A. Valentine/Ipswich Transport Museum)

SERVICES 2/2A

At the junction of Nacton Road and Clapgate Lane, which is on the right, Karrier 111 is about to pass under an overhead trailing junction on a return from Priory Heath to the town centre in August 1962; Clapgate Lane was the preserve of Services 6A and 6B. The powered overhead turnout junction can be seen top left, with the driver's direction setting indicator mounted half way up the supporting traction standard.

(A. Gordon collection)

This imposing passenger shelter was erected at the junction of the two roads seen in the last picture, with Sunbeam 118 about to leave for Electric House. A short distance to the rear of 118 was where Service 2A left Hatfield Road to join Nacton Road, and then onwards to Priory Heath, and subsequently the Airport.

(G. Lumb)

At the same location, Karrier 113 passes a sister vehicle outward bound towards Priory Heath. The passenger shelter still exists. (G. Lumb)

SERVICES 2/2A

This smart conductor stands beside Ransomes 22 at Derby Road Station, which was the original terminus of Service 2 when first opened in June 1926. The service was subsequently extended to Rands Way/Kings Way in March 1928 and eventually became Service 2A. At the time the photograph was taken, the return was across town to Bramford Road. Note the solid wheel and tyre, which was subsequently changed to pneumatic format.
(Author's collection)

Leading on from Derby Road Station, this is a rare view of a vehicle in Hatfield Road as Sunbeam 122 travels towards the junction with Nacton Road on 16th April 1955. Only vehicles on Service 2A to Priory Heath, and subsequently the Airport, used Hatfield Road, with 122's destination blind indicating the former on this occasion.
(P. Mitchell)

SERVICES 2/2A

With the Clapgate Lane junction on the left, Karrier 114 continues along Nacton Road as Service 2 to the Airport, with a sister vehicle following in the distance on Service 6B to Gainsborough. (P. Mitchell)

Sunbeam 121 is depicted outside what is now the Murrayside Community Centre, Nacton Road on 14th October 1961, en route to the Airport displaying Service 2. In the distance is the junction with Hatfield Road, which was used by the original Airport Service 2A. (P. Mitchell)

SERVICES 2/2A

Intending passengers wait to board Karrier 111 outside the erstwhile Racecourse Hotel, which was located at the junction of Nacton and Benacre Roads. The hotel name originates from the fact that the old racecourse (1711 – 1911) finishing line was close by. The hotel was demolished in 2009 and replaced with apartments; currently the lower floor is a Tesco Express convenience store.
(A. Valentine/Ipswich Transport Museum)

In this snowy scene, Karrier 110 moves along Nacton Road as it passes Rands Way on the right.
(A. Valentine/Ipswich Transport Museum)

At roughly the same location Karrier W 107 passes Landseer Road on the left, and Rands Way to the right, as it moves along Nacton Road towards the Priory Heath terminus. The wiring along Landseer Road was used by the original Service 6 to Gainsborough, but at the time the photograph was taken was providing access for workmen and school specials, plus depot runs. In the early days, Rands Way and Kings Way were wired to the junction with Felixstowe Road, but later only used for electrical supply purposes.
(A. Valentine/Ipswich Transport Museum)

SERVICES 2/2A

Looking in the opposite direction, Karrier W 101 is returning from Priory Heath on 16th May 1959, and passes the end of Landseer Road on the right, and Rands Way opposite, as it moves along Nacton Road. Note the police box on the left; these were usually painted blue.
(P. Mitchell)

Local authority housing stock provides the backdrop for this snowy scene of Sunbeam 115 approaching the Priory Heath terminus. The contact for the automatic operation of the overhead junction into Lindbergh Road can be seen on the nearside wire adjacent to the traction standard to the rear of 115.
(A. Valentine/Ipswich Transport Museum)

SERVICES 2/2A

Karrier 114 negotiates the Priory Heath overhead wiring as it leaves Nacton Road to enter Lindbergh Road to reach the Cobham Road depot on 23rd August 1963, the last day of trolleybus operation. The side panel has been suitably inscribed, and this day ended virtually 60 years of electrically powered public transport provided by the trams and trolleybuses. The Vernon's pool prize of £120,316 would be worth circa £1,756,000 today!
(Author's collection)

Sunbeam 116 begins the turn round at Priory Heath, with Lindbergh Road on the left leading to Cobham Road and the depot.
(A. Belton)

SERVICES 2/2A

Here we see Sunbeam 115 completing the turn back at the junction of Lindbergh Road.
(A. Valentine/Ipswich Transport Museum)

Looking towards the Airport Sunbeam 116 has almost completed the turn round ready for the return to the town centre.
(A. Belton)

Having completed the turn using the Priory Heath terminal wiring on 16th June 1962, Karrier W 107 is ready to return to the town centre, although the destination blind still needs to be changed to reflect this. (P. Mitchell)

On a gloomy winters' day, Massey bodied Ransomes 75 looks in a pretty well-worn state as it waits for passengers, having turned at the Priory Heath terminus before returning to Electric House via Nacton Road and Bishops Hill. The photograph was taken before the extension of wiring further along Nacton Road on the left to the Airport in 1947. (Remember When)

This picture, which appears to have been taken on the same winter's day seen in the previous view, depicts Ransomes 12 waiting to return across town to Adair Road as Service 8 via Derby and St John's Roads and the town centre. 12 entered service in 1926, and lasted until 1949, an outstanding 23 years, although with some rebuilding during this period. (Remember When)

SERVICES 2/2A

The Priory Heath terminus had a heavy concentration of overhead wiring, which was somewhat overpowering. In addition to providing a turning facility, vehicles could travel in any of two directions. Karrier 111 continues along Nacton Road towards the Airport; note the full width bridging pole behind 111 carrying the overhead wiring.
(A. Valentine/Ipswich Transport Museum)

On the approach to the Airport terminus on Nacton Road, and outside the factory of Crane Fluid Systems, two vehicles are on display whilst engaged on enthusiast specials in July 1949. In the foreground is the unique Massey bodied Ransomes 86, followed by Karrier 111. Crane were manufacturers of valves and pipe fittings, and after producing various military items during the Second World War, returned to producing its own products employing nearly 2000 personnel. The site is now occupied by the Futura Retail Park, which includes Waitrose and John Lewis stores.
(A. Gordon collection)

Shift change at the Crane factory in August 1963 with employees waiting for Karrier 111, fitted with a couple of new side panels, to make the Airport turn back to the town centre. (P. Mitchell)

The Airport terminus was opposite the entrance to the Crane factory, from which a Fordson lorry is emerging. Wiring was extended along Nacton Road from Lindbergh Road in 1947, and in this view Karrier W 108, displaying Service 2A, waits to return to the town centre in July 1949. The airport facility was to the right of this picture, and was owned by Ipswich Corporation, having opened in 1930. Various elements of the RAF used the airfield during the Second World War, and post war the main users were Channel Airways, Suckling Airways and Hawk Air. The airport was delicenced in December 1996, and is now covered by the Ravenswood housing estate.
(A. Gordon collection)

SERVICES 2/2A

On what appears to be the final trolleybus journey from the Airport on the 23rd August 1963, the last day of the system, Karrier 114 is depicted bedecked in bunting to mark the occasion. On return to the town centre 114 made the final trolleybus working to the Priory Heath depot. The nearside bulkhead window is open, which seemed to be a common practice on the Ipswich system. Note the sun visor above the windscreens, a feature unique to Ipswich's post war Park Royal bodied vehicles, and seen more frequently on southern hemisphere systems.
(A. Valentine/Ipswich Transport Museum)

Having completed the terminal manoeuvre, Sunbeam 115, showing an incorrect destination display, departs along Nacton Road back to the town centre in August 1962. The terminal wiring seen in the background featured on a catalogue cover of overhead equipment supplier, British Insulated Callender's Cables (BICC).
(A. Gordon collection)

SERVICES 3/3A and 9/9A

3 WHITTON – NORWICH RD – ELECTRIC HOUSE – WOODBRIDGE RD – RUSHMERE HEATH
3A WHITTON – NORWICH RD – ELECTRIC HOUSE – LATTICE BARN (SHORT WORKING)
9 RUSHMERE HEATH – WOODBRIDGE RD – CORNHILL – NORWICH RD – WHITTON
9A RUSHMERE HEATH – WOODBRIDGE RD – CORNHILL – NORWICH RD BRIDGE
(SHORT WORKING)

Service 3

9/6/26	Tram service along Spring Road to Lattice Barn replaced by trolleybus. Departure Cornhill.
25/4/34	Extended along Woodbridge Road East to Rushmere Heath (Playford Road). Lattice Barn retained as a short working (**Service 3A**). Removed circa 1957.
??/7/47	Departure moved to Electric House. Return as **Service 9** to Cornhill.
28/4/62	Last Day. Replaced by motorbus.

Service 9

27/7/26	Tram service to Whitton replaced by trolleybus. Departure Cornhill.
8/8/33	Short working at junction with Cromer Road (Norwich Road Bridge **Service 9A**).
??/7/47	Return as **Service 3** to Electric House.
28/4/62	Last day. Replaced by motorbus.

With booms at full stretch, Karrier 114 negotiates the road works on the approach to the Whitton terminus having arrived from Rushmere Heath as Service 9. The Maypole Inn is to the immediate left. (A. Belton)

SERVICE 3/3A

Karrier W 104 begins the tight turn at the Whitton terminus, located next to The Maypole Inn in June 1960. This was not an ideal location as evidenced by the notice instructing pub customers to park in the yard to the rear. The notice also indicates a "Tram Turning Circle"; many passengers continued to refer to trolleybuses as trams. (C. Carter)

Sunbeam 126 waits in the turning circle whilst on an enthusiasts' tour. The smaller notice also directs the players of the local football club, and supporters, to the rear of the pub to ensure the circle area is kept clear for turning trolleybuses. (D. Pearson)

SERVICE 3/3A

Karrier 114 leaves the Whitton terminus to return to Rushmere Heath as Service 3. Metal plate advertisements for Lyons' cakes are prominent on the building in the background. (A. Belton)

A Ransomes built vehicle, purchased to evaluate the local manufacturer's product before placing a bulk order, has completed the Whitton turn back. The destination indicator shows a return to Lloyds Avenue, which is strange as this thoroughfare was not wired until prior to the introduction of the one-way system along Tavern and Westgate Streets in 1949. The probable explanation is that during the period of the Royal Show in 1934, wiring was erected from Hyde Park Corner to what eventually would become Electric House. It was used by a service from here to Whitton in order to take pressure off the heavy loadings in the Cornhill because of the Show, and the nearest terminal thoroughfare was Lloyds Avenue. It provided a turning facility in the town centre, which did not exist as at that time all services were cross town. (Author's collection)

SERVICE 3/3A

Having completed the turn back in April 1956, in the foreground is pre-war Massey bodied Ransomes 76 on an enthusiasts' tour, followed by Karrier W 97, with the destination blind set for the return across town to Rushmere Heath as Service 3. The pub sign is on the extreme left; the substantial telegraph pole is not something that is seen very often in today's road scene.
(A. Gordon collection)

With the Maypole Inn public house on the left, Sunbeam 115 leads three vehicles at the Whitton terminus on 8th June 1957. Note the tramway style finial topping the traction standard on the left.
(P. Mitchell)

In June 1957 Karrier 113 negotiates around a fallen tree and broken overhead wiring in Norwich Road, with a policeman in attendance. To achieve this manoeuvre the booms are being transferred to the inward overhead wiring. (Ipswich Transport Museum)

Weymann bodied Karrier W 89, destined for Rushmere Heath on Service 3, will shortly approach the regular Cromer Road short working facility whilst travelling along Norwich Road on 8th June 1957. Large telegraph poles again feature in this image, and an AA patrol motorcyclist follows close behind. (P. Mitchell)

SERVICE 3/3A

Karrier W 108 has just passed under the railway bridge as it moves along Norwich Road on return to Rushmere Heath as Service 3; the bridge carries the track to the Felixstowe and East Suffolk lines. Beyond the bridge was the short working terminus of Service 9A located at the junction with Cromer Road. Dales Road leads off bottom right. (A. Belton)

With the Valley Road junction in the background, Sunbeam 122 rounds the bend in Norwich Road en route to Rushmere Heath. When this photograph was taken, also on the 8th June 1957, the junction was controlled by traffic lights, but now features two small adjacent traffic islands. (P. Mitchell)

Karrier W 107 is about to leave Norwich Road at Barrack Corner to enter St Matthews Street on 25th September 1960, with Barrack Lane on the right. The actual barracks were along the latter, and were erected circa 1796; the first occupants were the Queen's Dragoon Guards. The site was sold to Ipswich Corporation in 1929, and demolished a year later to make way for social housing. (P. Mitchell)

Also at Barrack Corner, Karrier W 103 rounds the bend out of Norwich Road into St Matthews Street in April 1953 when returning from Whitton, and with the destination blind set for Service 3 to Rushmere Heath. The overhead wiring middle left leads into London Road, and that on the extreme left into Portman Road, formerly known as Mill Street. On the right is the Half Moon and Star public house. (A. Gordon collection)

SERVICE 3/3A

At Barrack Corner, Weymann bodied Karrier W 90 moves into Norwich Road from St Matthews Street, with Barrack Lane on the left. The Half Moon and Star public house provides the back drop; the premises are now a private residence. (W. J. Haynes)

At the stop in St Matthews Street, Sunbeam 117 will shortly enter Barracks Corner, and then onwards to Norwich Road on 25th September 1960. Note the queuing corridors painted on the pavement. The surgical appliance store is not shy of advertising its wares; a Ford car passes an Austin Cambridge parked outside the premises. (P. Mitchell)

This view looks along Westgate Street, now pedestrianised, from the Cornhill, which was taken before the introduction of the one-way system in 1949. An unidentified Massey bodied Ransomes approaches the Cornhill whilst negotiating the street's narrowness for two-way traffic. Overhead wiring from the far left is from Princes Street, followed by that from Tavern Street; just out of view on the right is the junction for wiring into Princes Street. (Author's collection)

Pre-war Massey bodied Ransomes 78 waits at the Cornhill stand before departing to Whitton on Service 9. (R. Wellings)

SERVICE 3/3A

87 was one of four utility vehicles which arrived in 1944 based on Karrier W (W signifying a wartime specification) chassis and Weymann bodies; they were fitted with wooden slatted seats. 87 has arrived from Rushmere Heath along Tacket Street to the rear, which is now pedestrianised, and is waiting on stand before departing for Whitton against the background of a scaffolded Lloyds building. Note the signs for local public facilities hanging from ornate ironwork. (A, M. Wright)

Sunbeam 123 waits before setting off for Whitton in July 1960 against the background of the original Post Office, and Victorian town hall building on the right. The latter is now used as a function centre and arts venue, whilst the Post Office is currently being fitted out as a restaurant. A range of period cars complete the picture with the three on the right comprising a Triumph Mayflower, Ford Anglia and a Morris Minor. The area is now pedestrianised with sequenced water spouts, greatly enjoyed by younger children on warmer days. (C. Carter)

Sunbeam 118 waits on the stand used by vehicles arriving from Princes Street on the right, having arrived from the Station or Bourne Bridge, and surrounded by a vast number of intending passengers. A queuing corridor can be seen painted on the island platform on the left.
(A. Belton)

On the north side of the Electric House town centre terminus (Crown Street), pre-war Ransomes 56 waits before travelling to Rushmere Heath on Service 3, having arrived from Whitton. This is one of the early double deckers which had the front elevation modified by the Corporation incorporating deeper windscreens. The Cricketers Hotel, now a Wetherspoons venue, provides the backdrop, and the parked Austin 7 completes the picture.
(R. Marshall/The Bus Archive)

SERVICE 3/3A

At the same location, Ransomes 49 waits before departing on the regular short working Service 3A to Lattice Barn in August 1950.
(C. Carter)

Ipswich was unusual in operating only trolleybuses until 1950, when the first six AEC Regents with Park Royal bodies were delivered, which signalled the beginning of the decline in electric public transport in the town. AEC 1 from this initial delivery is seen here on the north side of Electric House (Crown Street) about to depart to Rushmere Heath.
(A. Valentine/Ipswich Transport Museum)

Also, on the north side of Electric House in October 1961, Karrier 110 waits before moving forward into the short St Margaret's Plain, and then St Margaret's Street leading to Majors Corner. The used car showroom in Tower Street on the right is now a Yates public house, and the period cars are parked on what is now the bus station. Note the unusual advertisements either side of the rear destination, and the rear of a Standard Vanguard car parked on the extreme left.

(J. C. Gillham)

This picture depicts a busy Cornhill in the early 1950s judging by the lady's fashions. This period can actually be confirmed as the scene incorporates the one-way system referred to earlier, introduced in 1949, and Ransomes 54 or 64 waiting to depart to Whitton was withdrawn in 1956. The long established Grimwade's clothing store takes centre stage, with "School Outfitters" advertised on the sun blind. On the upper storey is an advertisement for Fina Petroleum Products, who merged with Total in 1999.

(Commercial postcard/F. W. Pawsey)

Mid-afternoon, roughly ten years later, Karrier 110 has just passed under the overhead crossover for wiring leading out from under the Lloyds Avenue arch into Princes Street. On the left is an AEC Regent on the replacement for trolleybus Service 8, which was extended into the White House Estate. By the time this photograph was taken, a passing loop in the overhead wiring to the right of 110 had been removed.

(J. C. Gillham)

Karrier W 108 has left St Margaret's Street under nearside overhead wiring at Majors Corner, and is about to enter St Helens Street. Botwoods garage and car showroom is to the right; note the blue painted police box, and the dark blue British Railways sign indicating the way to the station.

(A. Belton)

Sunbeam 118 moves along St Helens Street on an outward journey to Rushmere Heath on 31st May 1958. On the left, a lorry emerges from Milner Street, now incorporated into Rope Walk. Following is a Standard 8 and a Hillman Husky.
(P. Mitchell)

Karrier W 107 descends Spring Road towards St Helens Street having passed under the high railway viaduct on 25th September 1960, which carried the line from Westerfield Junction to Felixstowe. The structure was built in 1876, comprising three arches 70ft high. It was financed by Colonel George Tomlin of Orwell Park, who was instrumental in Felixstowe's development.
(P. Mitchell)

SERVICE 9

Having just passed Cauldwell Hall Road, Sunbeam 116 continues along Spring Road destined for Whitton on 16th May 1959.
(P. Mitchell)

In January 1953, Karrier W 101 collided with a traction standard in Spring Road. AEC tower wagon PV 8580 is in attendance with a tow rope attached ready to pull the vehicle away from the damaged traction standard.
(Ipswich Transport Museum)

This incident involving a Ford Prefect in Spring Road at the junction with Cowper Street has attracted a large crowd as Massey bodied Ransomes 75 waits to pass the obstruction. The shop on the left is now a Funeral Directors, and the pub opposite on the corner of Milton Street has made way for a fast-food outlet. Note the large telegraph pole. (Ipswich Transport Museum)

Having just left the Rushmere Heath terminus, AEC Regent 6 from the original 1950 motorbus delivery moves along Woodbridge Road East en route to Whitton on 14th October 1961. Behind the unseen property on the right is the Ipswich Hospital site. (P. Mitchell)

Karrier W 105 leaves Woodbridge Road East, and enters Playford Road before turning back towards the town centre at the Rushmere Heath terminus, and then onwards to Whitton as Service 9.

(A. Valentine/Ipswich Transport Museum)

At the Rushmere Heath terminus on 14th October 1961, AEC Regent 2 from the first batch of trolleybus replacement vehicles, waits to return back to Whitton on Service 9.

(P. Mitchell)

SERVICE 3/3A

At the same location, Karrier W 101 awaits departure, with the driver relaxing on the downstairs bench seat. The lower side panels on these semi-utility vehicles were painted as they were steel, as opposed to the burnished aluminium panels of pre- and post-war vehicles. (R. L. Wilson/ Online Transport Archive)

A coloured view of Karrier 112 on layover at the Rushmere Heath terminus, with the destination blind yet to be changed to Service 9 for the return to Whitton. The ornate shelter is no more. Further along Playford Road on the right are the current Ipswich Town Football Club training facilities.
(G. Lumb)

Ransomes 6 is seen here in Woodbridge Road having left the Rushmere Heath terminus on the left. It is thought that this is the very first working of this service on 25th April 1934. Note the crew's summer uniform, the bulb horn and the destination set for one of the earlier cross-town services to the Station. A Ransomes demonstrator was also allocated fleet number 6 during its four months stay between December 1925 and April 1926. (Ipswich Transport Museum)

SERVICE 4
TOWN CENTRE – BISHOPS HILL – FELIXSTOWE ROAD – ST AUGUSTINE'S

27/5/26	Tram service along Felixstowe Road to the Royal Oak (Derby Road) replaced by trolleybus and extended to Kings Way. Departure/return Cornhill.
18/3/28	Linked with **Service 2** from Kings Way. From here onwards to town centre via Nacton and St John's Roads, then retrace routes above. Destination display was Rands Way although no turning facility was available
6/12/36	Extended from Kings Way to St Augustine's Church at junction with Bixley Road. Initially absorbed into **Circular Services 0** and not **Service 2**. Departure/return to Electric House.
23/3/39	Link with **Service 2** reintroduced.
9/12/51	The above ceased. Now terminated at St Augustine's church
23/8/63	Last day. Replaced by motorbus.

Sunbeam 116 has just turned out of Tower Street, the eastern side of the Electric House terminus, and waits to reach the stand for Service 4 to St Augustine's. The side advertisement relates to a long established Ipswich furniture business, which closed its town centre premises in 2014 to consolidate activities at its Relax store in Bramford Road. (Author's collection)

SERVICE 4

Karrier 114 passes Sunbeam 115, with the latter destined for St Augustine's, and 114 on the short working to Kingsway, for the Priory Heath depot. A British Railways Scammell Scarab on local deliveries brings up the rear. (A. Belton)

Looking along the south side of the Electric House terminus, we see Karrier 114 turning into the west side, to then pass the Cricketers Hotel in the background as it leaves for St Augustine's. To the rear is sister vehicle 111 destined for Gainsborough on Service 6A; the passing loop of overhead wiring can be seen above. Note the play on words in the Guinness advertisement. (D. Pearson)

SERVICE 4

This photograph features four of the major buildings that surround the town centre Electric House terminus, with the named building centre stage. On the extreme left is the three storey Tower Ramparts school, and next the original Odeon cinema, now a Bingo venue. To the right of Karrier W 107 destined for St Augustine's, is the Cricketers Hotel. By the time this photograph was taken in June 1963 the overhead wiring that allowed parallel running in front of the hotel, and provided access to the stands outside the school, had been removed.

(J. C. Gillham)

Karrier 110 turns out of Crown Street into Tower Street to reach the north side terminal stand on 16th June 1962. The splicing ears in the overhead wires indicate where there was a trailing junction for wiring coming from just above the AEC motorbus. The latter is advertising Butlin's Clacton Summer Season.

(P. Mitchell)

Sunbeam 123 passes the policeman on point duty in St Margaret's Street as it approaches the junction with Woodbridge Road, which is to the left of the advertising hoardings, beyond which the second Odeon cinema was built. The left-hand wiring from the automatic overhead turnout junction top left was originally for Woodbridge Road, but by the time this photograph was taken in October 1961, wiring along this road had been removed. In this view, the left-hand wiring now leads into St Helen's Street at Majors Corner, replacing an overhead turn out nearer this junction. To the left of 123, local brewer Tolly Cobbold's lorry waits to leave St Margaret's Green.
(J. C. Gillham)

With Botwoods garage and workshop on the left, Karrier 112 leaves Majors Corner on return from St Augustine's, and moves towards the bus stop in the foreground. Note the intending female passengers are all wearing head scarves, something rarely seen in today's fashion scene
(A.Valentine/Ipswich Transport Museum)

SERVICE 4

Looking in the opposite direction towards St. Margaret's Street Sunbeam 115 is about to leave Majors Corner to enter Upper Orwell Street under offside overhead wiring. (A. Belton)

SERVICE 4

At the same location Karrier 110 carries out the same manoeuvre. The clock advertising Austin Service had lost it's hands.
(A. Belton)

Karrier 109 leaves the narrow Upper Orwell Street at Majors Corner to enter St Margaret's Street in June 1963, and thence to Electric House. The between deck advertisement is for the local brewer, and following close behind is a Big Bedford lorry. The supermarket on the corner is now occupied by the Papa Chinese Restaurant and Bar.
(J. C. Gillham)

Looking in the opposite direction in August 1961, the narrowness of Upper Orwell Street is emphasised as Sunbeam 121 makes towards Fore Street, and onwards to St Augustine's. In the background, a second vehicle leaves Majors Corner with Botwoods car showroom beyond; the site is now the car park for the Regent Theatre. The Rover taxi on the left carries Licence Number 185.

(A. Gordon collection)

Karrier W 107 moves along Upper Orwell Street, with St Michael's Parish Church in the background. Many of the properties on the right have been replaced with more modern buildings, or have received facelifts.

(A. Valentine/Ipswich Transport Museum)

This driver's cab view emphasises the narrowness of Fore Street at this point as Karrier 111 makes its way towards the dock area. The premises of Martin and Newby are again in view.

(A. Valentine/Ipswich Transport Museum)

Moving further along Upper Orwell Street, Karrier 112 picks up the waiting passengers on 14th October 1961. Note the barrow on the left with the owner selling vegetables priced by using the scales with individual metal weights.
(P. Mitchell)

Having left Upper Orwell Street, Karrier 110 has entered the narrow Fore Street leading down to the dock area. It will shortly cross Star Lane, and move onwards to the junction with Duke Street and Fore Hamlet. One of the AEC Regent motorbuses that replaced the trolleybuses travels in the opposite direction.
(A. Valentine/Ipswich Transport Museum)

SERVICE 4

Looking along Fore Street towards the Duke Street/Fore Hamlet junction, Karrier 114 leads a selection of period cars back to the town centre. On the left is The Lord Nelson public house, which dates back to the 1600s, and was previously known as The Noah's Ark. The pub is advertising Tolly Ales, the business resulting from the amalgamation of two local family brewers, namely Tollemache and Cobbold. (D. Pearson)

On what appears to be a warm day, Karrier W 102 leaves Fore Hamlet to navigate the traffic island at the Duke Street junction; the island has recently been removed and replaced with traffic lights. The building in the background is St Clement's Congregational church, which has now been converted into apartments. It was unusual for a congregational church to carry a saint's name, but this actually referred to the local Ipswich parish. Note the advertisement for the local brewers. (S. Lockwood collection)

SERVICE 4

With the Gardeners Arms public house on the right, Karrier 112 is about to leave Fore Hamlet to begin the ascent of Bishops Hill. (A. Belton)

SERVICE 4

Looking in the opposite direction, Karrier W 106 has completed the descent of Bishops Hill on the return to Electric House. Cavendish Street leads off to the left.
(A. Valentine/Ipswich Transport Museum)

112 is seen again climbing Bishops Hill towards the junction with Nacton Road. The cyclist and the scooter owner are obviously enjoying the hospitality of the White Elm public house.
(A. Valentine/Ipswich Transport Museum)

At the top of Bishops Hill, Sunbeam 115 will continue along Felixstowe Road to St Augustine's. Overhead wiring off to the left leads into Nacton Road.
(A. Valentine/Ipswich Transport Museum)

SERVICE 4

The steepness of Bishops Hill has beaten the three cyclists as Karrier 109 descends towards Fore Hamlet. An Austin A30 or A35 follows close behind on 28th June 1963. (P. Mitchell)

Karrier 111 is approaching the junction with Nacton Road as it moves along Felixstowe Road before dropping down Bishops Hill to Fore Hamlet and Fore Street in August 1961. Ransomes trolleybuses produced for other customers were tested along this stretch of road, presumably to check performance up the steep Bishops Hill. In today's environment one would not leave a bicycle at the side of the road, as seen to the rear of 111.
(A. Gordon collection)

SERVICE 4

Felixstowe Road stretches back towards Bishops Hill as Karrier W 106, seen adjacent to Levington Road, makes its way to St Augustine's under cantilevered bracket arm suspended wiring. Note the unusual sewing machine advertisements either side of the front destination display. (A. Valentine/Ipswich Transport Museum)

With the Royal Oak public house, now closed, providing the backdrop, 106 is seen again as it continues along Felixstowe Road, and crosses the junction with Derby Road on the right, and Hatfield Road opposite. Overhead wiring along these two roads crossed that in Felixstowe Road at 75 degrees, and was used by Service 2A to the Airport, but this had been removed by the time this photograph was taken. A Co-op battery electric delivery van follows close behind. (A. Valentine/Ipswich Transport Museum)

Under 18" spaced overhead wiring, 106 puts in another appearance whilst moving along Felixstowe Road, and having just passed the end of King Edward Road on the right. (A. Valentine/Ipswich Transport Museum)

SERVICE 4

Looking outwards towards Kings Way on 16th May 1959, 106 is seen yet again, with a Ford Anglia following, returning to Electric House from St Augustine's, with Hatfield Road off to the right. The building on the left no longer exists. (P. Mitchell)

SERVICE 4

Having crossed the bridge over the railway line to Felixstowe on leaving St Augustine's, Karrier 112 passes the junction with Cobham Road and Kings Way as it continues along Felixstowe Road. The overhead wiring off to the right leads into Cobham Road, and the Priory Heath trolleybus depot that is now the site of the Ipswich Transport Museum. This junction was the original Kings Way terminus before the extension to St Augustine's church. The 15 degree overhead turnout top left is much larger, and heavier, than the more common 25 degree installation. (A. Valentine/Ipswich Transport Museum)

Sunbeam 118 has also crossed the railway bridge and is about to pass under a crossover carrying wiring from Cobham Road on 14th October 1961. Following close behind is an Austin 7, and the tower of St Augustine's church is on the horizon. (P. Mitchell)

A short working to Kings Way was used to gain access to the Cobham Road depot, and Karrier W 107 is depicted here about to enter on 13th May 1963; the Kings Way/Felixstowe Road junction with Cobham Road is in the distance. The trailing overhead junction out of Wright Road can be seen top left. (P. Mitchell)

With St Augustine's church in the background, Karrier 111 has left the terminus, and begins the climb up the incline leading to the bridge over the railway line to Felixstowe on 16th June 1962. The Cobham Road depot is roughly a quarter of a mile to the right on the other side of the railway cutting. (P. Mitchell)

SERVICE 4

Sunbeam 123 begins the turn back to the town centre with Bixley Road in the background, from which overhead wiring for the circular services had been removed by the time this photograph was taken on 14th October 1961.
(P. Mitchell)

Karrier W 106 rounds the terminal traffic island on 16th May 1959 to reach the layover stand in Felixstowe Road, before returning to Electric House. On the left overhead wiring enters the island from Bixley Road, which was used by the clockwise circular Service O; there was wiring in the opposite direction for the anti-clockwise circular service.
(P. Mitchell)

SERVICE 4

At the St Augustine's terminus, with the imposing named church in the background, Sunbeam 125 has circumnavigated the traffic island to the rear in August 1961. 125 will travel a short distance along Felixstowe Road to cross the railway to the named resort, and then arrive at the junction with Cobham Road and Kings Way. (A. Gordon collection)

SERVICE 5
TOWN CENTRE – ST HELENS STREET – GROVE LANE – FOXHALL ROAD

22/12/26	Service opened as far as Derby Road station. Departure/return Cornhill.
29/3/27	Extended further along Foxhall Road to a terminus adjacent to Heath Lane.
13/12/36	Extended a short distance to join new wiring along Bixley and Heath Roads.
By 1936	Linked cross town with Station (**Service X**) or Bourne Bridge (**Service 1**).
??/7/49	Departure moved to Electric House via Princes St, Portman Rd, Barrack Corner, Crown St.
??/??/51	Cross town links ceased.
??/12/51	Departure from Electric House reached via Westgate St., Hyde Park Corner and Crown St.
31/5/58	Last day. Replaced by motorbus.

Weymann bodied utility Karrier W 89 waits on the north side of the Electric House terminus (Crown Street) before leaving for Foxhall Road. Beyond is the area covered by the multitude of period cars, now occupied by the bus station, and the Tower Ramparts School, which has been replaced by a shopping centre, originally carrying the same name, but now called Sailmakers. To the right is the first Odeon cinema building at the top of Lloyds Avenue, now a Mecca Bingo Hall. (R. Marshall/The Bus Archive)

At the same location, with the Cricketers Hotel as the backdrop, Massey bodied Ransomes 85 waits before leaving on an outward journey. The driver appears to be having a conversation with someone through the open near side cab door. (A. Valentine/Ipswich Transport Museum

A spot of bother at the same location providing contrasting rear views. The linesman of AEC tower wagon PV8580 is attending to the overhead junction of the parallel wiring, with Sunbeam 121 destined for Foxhall Road immediately behind. At the rear 89 is seen again, with the driver transferring the booms to the right hand wiring to be able to pass the vehicle in front. (J. H. Meredith/Online Transport Archive)

SERVICE 5

Karrier 109 begins the sharp climb up Grove Lane on 31st May 1958, having left the St Helens Street/Spring Road junction in the distance. A Morris Minor is parked in Oxford Road on the left. (P. Mitchell)

Having almost reached the top of the incline on the same day, Sunbeam 119 will shortly leave Grove Lane to join Foxhall Road at the junction with Back Hamlet. Note the Trolley Bus Stop sign on the left. (P. Mitchell)

Under 18" spaced overhead wiring, Karrier 114 moves along Foxhall Road as it passes the end of Fuchsia Lane on 31st May 1958, just before reaching the junction with Derby Road. The corner shop has the usual tobacco advertisements, and the widow display is protected from the sun by a side blind in addition to the normal overhead cover. A Ford Consul follows close behind. (P. Mitchell)

Also, on the same day as above, the lone Massey bodied Ransomes 86 continues past the end of Henslow Road, with Foxhall Road stretching back to the Derby Road/Cauldwell Hall Road junction in the distance. (P. Mitchell)

SERVICE 5

Sunbeam 119 is about to approach the terminal roundabout at the junction of Heath and Bixley Roads on 31st May 1958. On the nearside overhead wiring, the contact to operate the three automatic overhead turnouts positioned around the traffic island can be seen. (P. Mitchell)

Pre-war Massey bodied Ransomes 83 is about to pass under the second automatic turnout as it circumnavigates the traffic island on 16th April 1955. The driver's direction indicator for the turnout can be seen on the adjacent traction standard; Bixley Road is off to the immediate right. (P. Mitchell)

Karrier W 93 navigates the traffic island at the junction of Heath Road on the left beyond the shrubbery, and Bixley Road behind the photographer's position. The overhead wiring along these two roads was used by the clockwise/anti-clockwise Service O circulars. This view was the basis of a winter scene painting by transport artist Malcolm Root, and subsequently published as a card by Rothbury Publishing. (S. E. Letts)

Karrier W 106 has completed the turnround, and moves to reach the stand for the return to the town centre on 16th April 1955. The first of the automatic turnouts, which leads into Heath Road, can be seen on the left with the driver's direction indicator light mounted on the adjacent traction standard. The town centre destination is shown as Cornhill, and to reach the Electric House north side departure stand, 106 will have to travel along Westgate Street, and make a right hand turn at Hyde Park Corner into Crown Street. (P. Mitchell)

SERVICES 6/6A/6B
TOWN CENTRE – GAINSBOROUGH

28/7/31	**Service 6** opened via Nacton and Landseer Roads terminating at Reynolds Road via a "round the houses" loop. Departure/return Cornhill
6/12/36	Departure/return moved to Electric House.
30/1/38	Extended along Landseer Road to the junction with Holbrook Road.
26/2/40	Extended further along Landseer/Holywells Roads and Duke Street. Holbrook turning circle eventually removed. Service now operated as two circulars. **Service 6A** Outward via Holywells and Landseer Roads; return as below. **Service 6B** Outward via Nacton and Landseer Roads; return as above. Short workings continued to the Reynolds Road loop.
17/12/45	Clapgate Lane wired from Nacton Road to Landseer Road. **Services 6A/6B** now use the above in place of Nacton Road beyond Clapgate Lane.
9/12/51	**Service 6** discontinued.
23/5/54	Reynolds Road loop removed.
23/8/63	Last day. Replaced by motorbus.

Services 6A and 6B shared overhead wiring between Electric House and the Fore Street/ Duke Street junction

On a return trip from Gainsborough on Service 6B, Karrier 110 has arrived at Electric House, and is about to leave the eastern side of the Tower Ramparts car park. On the left, a Triumph Herald can be seen, together with the rear of a Ford Popular.
(A. Belton)

SERVICE 6A/6B

The towering structure of the Tower Ramparts School provides the backdrop for these three vehicles on the Electric House southern stands in July 1949. In the foreground, behind the crew members in their summer lightweight jackets, is Karrier W 98 destined for Gainsborough on Service 6B, with a pre-war Ransomes vehicle immediately behind. In the background, Karrier W 104 awaits departure on Service 11 to Sidegate Lane. The Tower Ramparts name now applies to the bus station sited on the left, and originally the shopping centre that replaced the school. The town's early rampart fortifications fringed the northern and eastern limits of the town. (A. Gordon collection)

SERVICE 6A/6B

On a wet day in June 1963, Karrier W 108 has left the Gainsborough stand outside the school, and is about to leave the western side of Electric House to join Crown Street. 108 is on the anticlockwise Service 6A to Gainsborough, leaving the shared wiring with the clockwise Service 6B at the Fore Street/Duke Street junction. (J. C. Gillham)

The extent of the Egerton building is illustrated in this view, with Karrier 111 passing the entrance to the fuel pumps. (A. Valentine/Ipswich Transport Museum)

The Kenning Self Motoring building, now demolished, stretches back along St Margaret's Street as Sunbeam 115 moves towards the junction with Woodbridge Road. The ghostly image of St Margaret's church can be seen in the background, with the entrance to the Manor House Ballroom on the right, which is now also a Social Club. (A. Valentine/Ipswich Transport Museum)

Weymann bodied utility Karrier W 89 on Service 6A in 1950 appears to be without a driver when seen in Crown Street at the entrance to the Electric House terminus area. Normally Service 6A would have turned at Electric House, so perhaps 89 has come from the Constantine Road depot to take up service. The actual Electric House building is on the extreme left, from which the town's electrical supply and public transport were administrated from 1932. The sign over the doorway reads "Corporation Showroom" presumably providing for the sale of electrical domestic appliances. Note the external lighting above the RAC sign on the premises of Egerton.
(A. Gordon collection)

Sunbeam 116 has just passed the junction with Woodbridge Road as it moves towards Majors Corner, and with the Mulberry Tree public house on the right; the building is now occupied as a Kurdish cultural centre. Parked on the pavement is a Morris Commercial J type van, a model which was produced between 1948 and 1961.
(A. Valentine/Ipswich Transport Museum)

SERVICE 6A/6B

At roughly the same location Karrier 111 on Service 6A passes the cleared site for the second Odeon cinema. The building to the rear, seen in the previous picture, is next to the Ipswich AEC Regent motorbus. Note that the nearside overhead wiring into Spring Road had been removed by the time this photograph was taken. Not seen very often in today's road scene is the motorcycle and sidecar on the left, which in the 1950s provided many working class families with independent transport before the growth of post-war car ownership.

(A. Valentine/Ipswich Transport Museum)

The buildings of motor dealer Botwoods provide the backdrop as Sunbeam 121 moves through Majors Corner. The British Railway station direction sign mounted above the traffic lights can be seen again; the Botwoods building has made way for the Regent Theatre car park, and the site of the second Odeon cinema. (A. Belton)

SERVICE 6A/6B

A coloured view at the same location, as seen in the picture before last, has Sunbeam 115 on the clockwise 6B service. (Travel Lens Photographic)

On what appears to be a miserable cold day Karrier 109 has just left Majors Corner, seen in the background, and enters St Margaret's Street to reach Electric House. The current Regent Theatre building is on the left, and the open space eventually became the site of the second Odeon cinema.
(A.Valentine/Ipswich Transport Museum

Having left Majors Corner, Karrier W 108 pulls away from the stop at the beginning of St Margaret's Street heading back to Electric House. Note the period road signs on the left, one of which gives directions to the Ipswich Airport.
(A. Valentine/Ipswich Transport Museum)

SERVICE 6A/6B

Karrier 114 returns to the town centre in June 1963, and is about to leave the narrow Upper Orwell Street at Majors Corner, and turn into St Margaret's Street on the right. The Duke of Kent public house is on the right to the rear of 114, and the building on the left is now occupied by an estate agent. (J.C. Gillham)

Looking along the length of Upper Orwell Street towards Fore Street in August 1963, Karrier 111 is destined for Gainsborough on Service 6A having just passed St Michael's Parish Church. A later delivered AEC Regent passes in the opposite direction. (P. Mitchell)

SERVICE 6A/6B

This busy scene in Upper Orwell Street again emphasises the narrowness of some of the Ipswich streets, especially with the kerb side parked bicycles. Karrier 109 makes away to Majors Corner, and onwards to Electric House.
(A.Valentine/Ipswich Transport Museum)

Karrier W 108 moves along Fore Street towards the dock area having left Upper Orwell Street. The premises of Martin and Newby can be seen in the background, where all items of an ironmongery nature could be purchased; the business closed in 2004.
(A.Valentine/Ipswich Transport Museum)

Karrier 112 travels north along Fore Street, past the Christmas decorated specialist shop on the corner with Orwell Street. Note the unusual name of the shop owner; the premises are now a kabab shop. (A. Belton)

SERVICE 6A/6B

This view yet again emphasises the narrowness of this section of Fore Street as Karrier 109 is seen nearer the docks. The buildings on the left still exist, but those opposite have received a facelift.
(A. Valentine/Ipswich Transport Museum)

Having crossed Star Lane, Weymann bodied Karrier W 87 continues along Fore Street past the junction with Salthouse Street on Service 6A to Gainsborough via Duke Street. All the properties in the picture still exist, although the pavements have been widened to create a single roadway for buses and access. The newsagents on the right, with sun blind and tobacco advertisements, is now a private residence.
(A. Valentine/Ipswich Transport Museum)

On an outward 6A journey to Gainsborough, Karrier 113 moves along Fore Street towards the junction with Fore Hamlet and Duke Street; 113 will move into the latter to complete an anticlockwise circuit back to Electric House.
(A. Valentine/Ipswich Transport Museum)

SERVICE 6A/6B

With Fore Street in the background, Karrier 109 is about to enter the traffic island at the junction of Duke Street and Fore Hamlet on Service 6A. 109 is just about to pass under the contact to operate the automatic overhead turnout junction for the named thoroughfares. The malt houses on the left have been replaced by University of Suffolk buildings, and the area to the right now leads to the car park for the Suffolk New College. The latter was created in 2009 when the course content of the old Suffolk College was split between the New College for further education, and the University Campus of Suffolk. (A. Valentine/Ipswich Transport Museum)

In this view, Karrier W 106 is about to pass under the overhead turnout referred to in the last caption. This is where Services 6A and 6B go their separate ways, with 106 on Service 6A leaving to enter Duke Street on the left; Service 6B vehicles entered Fore Hamlet on the right. The two services will meet again on arrival at Gainsborough. (A. Valentine/Ipswich Transport Museum)

Service 6A Anti-clockwise Circuit

With the Fore Street/Fore Hamlet traffic island in the background, Karrier 112 has entered Duke Street to begin a 6A anti-clockwise circuit to Gainsborough on 14th October 1961, with a Mini close behind. The Suffolk College building can be seen in the distance, and a period road sign is to the left. (P. Mitchell)

On 16th May 1959, Karrier W 96 has left the bends out of John Street, which no longer exists, to join Holywells Road, and will immediately pass the erstwhile gas works on the left. (P. Mitchell)

SERVICE 6A

On a murky day, warranting the use of headlights in April 1962, Karrier 114 has left John Street and passes the old gas works, on an outward journey to Gainsborough. Today the condition of the road is much improved, and the area covered by the gas works now devoted to apartment blocks. (D. Pearson)

Having left Holywells Road, Karrier 113 Is seen on the concrete Landseer Road between Cliff Lane and Greenwich Close on a warm 28th August 1959 judging by the open windscreens. In the background, the top of a large German gasometer can be seen. (P. Mitchell)

SERVICE 6A

113 is seen again climbing the concrete section of Landseer Road towards Gainsborough in April 1962 under the overhead wiring erected in 1940 between Holbrook Road and Fore Street. On the left horizon is a crane located on Cliff Quay, the downriver dock area of the River Orwell, and on the lower land to the right is the major fuel depot adjacent to the quay. (D. Pearson)

Karrier 110 awaits departure back to Electric House from the Gainsborough 6A stand before turning into Clapgate Lane on the left, and travelling on the anti-clockwise circuit back to the town centre. (A. Belton)

Clapgate Lane, the domain of Services 6A and 6B, stretches into the distance towards Landseer Road as Karrier 111 is about to join Nacton Road on the return to the town centre. The passenger shelter referred to earlier is on the left. (G. Lumb/Travel Lens Photographic)

On a cold snowy day, Karrier 110 is about to descend Bishop's Hill having left Nacton Road in the right background. (A. Valentine/Ipswich Transport Museum)

SERVICE 6A

Sunbeam 115 approaches the end of a virtually empty Clapgate Lane, and will shortly join Nacton Road on the return to the town centre.
(A.Valentine/Ipswich Transport Museum)

The lone cyclist passes Karrier 113 at the Felixstowe Road end of Nacton Road. Note the two brackets below the nearside windscreen which allowed for slip boards to be used to identify school specials and workmen services in the 1950s.
(A. Valentine/Ipswich Transport Museum)

With the electricity sub-station in the background, Sunbeam 115 has completed the anti-clockwise circuit having just left Fore Hamlet to enter the traffic island leading into Fore Street. In addition to feeding the trolleybus system, the sub-station also fed the long forgotten industrial factories that were in the area. It is now occupied by The Forge Kitchen restaurant.
(A.Valentine/Ipswich Transport Museum)

Service 6B Clockwise Circuit

In August 1961, Sunbeam 119 has climbed the steep Bishops Hill, and is about to turn into Nacton Road, and onward to Clapgate Lane. An Austin lorry belonging to Mellonies Ltd, a local resurfacing contractor, follows close behind; in earlier years the company was a coal merchant in Ipswich. (C. W. Routh)

At the Nacton Road/Clapgate Lane junction, Karrier W 107 begins the turn into the latter with the driver using a hand signal in addition to the pivoting trafficator. A Standard Vanguard is on the extreme left of the picture.
(A. Valentine/Ipswich Transport Museum)

Making the same manoeuvre, Karrier 111 enters Clapgate Lane, and is about to pass under an overhead crossover. Note the electrical feed lines from the right hand traction standard next to Levington Road. (A. Valentine/Ipswich Transport Museum)

SERVICE 6B

Another view of the location seen at the top of the previous page depicts Karrier 109 about to enter Nacton Road in June 1963 having climbed Bishops Hill in the background. The destination display appears to be at the end of the blind reel, and a group of workmen toil up the incline with their bicycles. (J. C. Gillham)

A little further along Clapgate Lane, from the view seen in the middle of the previous page, Sunbeam 117 has just left Nacton Road in May 1962, and is about to leave the first fare stage stop in Clapgate Lane. The shelter referred to earlier can be seen again in the background. (A. Gordon collection)

SERVICE 6B

117 is seen again moving along Clapgate Lane past the end of Benacre Road on 16th May 1959 travelling outwards to Gainsborough.
(P. Mitchell)

With All Hallows Court on the left, Karrier 113 continues along Clapgate Lane on 23rd August 1959; it appears to be a warm day judging by the open nearside windscreen.
(P. Mitchell)

SERVICE 6B

Karrier W 108 passes a row of shops in Clapgate Lane on the approach to Landseer Road. The destination blind has been changed ready for the return to the town centre. The shops still exist, although under different ownership, and a Rover car crosses to the rear. (A. Valentine/Ipswich Transport Museum)

Sunbeam 118 turns out of Clapgate Lane to reach the Gainsborough terminal stand in Landseer Road. 118 will return to the town centre by continuing along Landseer Road, and then along Holywells Road and Duke Street. Overhead wiring to the right leading through to Nacton Road was used by the original Service 6, but by the time this photograph was taken it was only traversed by school specials, workmen services and depot runs.
(A. Valentine/Ipswich Transport Museum)

A coloured view of the terminal stand with Karrier 112 waiting to depart in a clockwise direction to Electric House via Holywells Road and Duke Street.
(Author's collection)

With the overhead wiring from Clapgate Lane in the background, Karrier 110 waits on stand in Landseer Road before returning to Electric House. To the rear, a Standard Vanguard emerges from the extension of Clapgate Lane. When the service to Gainsborough first opened, vehicles approached from Nacton Road, and turned left past the Standard car's position to follow a "round the houses" terminal loop via Cotman and Reynolds Roads. The facility was removed in 1954. (A. Gordon collection)

Karrier 113 and Sunbeam 118 wait at their respective Gainsborough stands before returning to Electric House on Services 6A and 6B. (A. Valentine/Ipswich Transport Museum)

SERVICE 6B

Looking in the opposite direction along Landseer Road in August 1961, two vehicles are both destined for a return to the town centre, but travelling in opposite directions. Karrier 110 will depart along Clapgate Lane (6A), and Sunbeam 125 will continue along Landseer Road to Holywells Road/ Duke Street (6B) before both re-joining at Fore Street. The original 1931 service into the Gainsborough Estate was extended a further half mile along Landseer Road to the junction with Holbrook Road in 1938, before completion of wiring to Fore Street in 1940.
(A. Gordon collection)

On 16th May 1959, Karrier W 97 continues the clockwise circuit back to Electric House, whilst in the distance a trolleybus waits on the stand seen in an earlier view.
(P. Mitchell)

SERVICE 6B

Sunbeam 117 passes All Hallows church, which is behind the trees, whilst moving along Landseer Road on a return trip to Electric House on 14th October 1961; to the left is Raeburn Road. (P. Mitchell)

A little further on, Karrier W 108 passes the continuation of Raeburn Road on the right, with a lorry emerging from the section of the road seen in the last picture. In the distance a Co-op battery electric delivery van can be seen on 28th June 1963. (P. Mitchell)

SERVICE 6B

Karrier 110 descends Landseer Road on 14th October 1961 with a return to the town centre. Close by was the Holbrook Road terminus used before the 1940 extension along Holywells Road and Duke Street to Fore Street. This terminal wiring was subsequently removed. (P. Mitchell)

Looking in the opposite direction, Karrier 110 descends Landseer Road towards Holywells Road under the final section of overhead wiring erected in 1940. On the left, groundwork is in hand on what is now an industrial site, and the large fuel storage depot can be seen on the right. (A. Gordon collection)

A large German gasometer dominates this scene as an unidentified vehicle leaves Holywells Road and turns towards John Street, which disappeared with the re-alignment of Duke Street. The occupants of the houses on the corner did not have a very pleasant view from their rear windows!

(A. Valentine/Ipswich Transport Museum)

In April 1962, Karrier W 108 travels along Holywells Road inward bound for Electric House past the industrial buildings adjacent to the earlier Eagle Corn Mills. In the background, the chimneys of the Cliff Quay power station can be seen; it was badly damaged by fire in 1982, and demolished in 1994, with thousands, including the author and his young son, watching the three chimneys collapse in unison. (D. Pearson)

With the electricity sub-station building on the left, Karrier W 103 is about to leave Duke Street and enter the junction with Fore Street and Fore Hamlet. Work is in hand to plant traction standards ready to modify the overhead wiring for the construction of a traffic island; in recent times it has reverted back from this to a junction, but now controlled by traffic lights. (A. Valentine/Ipswich Transport Museum)

SERVICE 7/7A

7 TOWN CENTRE – LONDON ROAD – CHANTRY PARK
7A TOWN CENTRE – LONDON ROAD – HADLEIGH ROAD LOOP

27/3/27	Service opened along London Road to Ranelagh Road. Departure/return Cornhill.
16/5/34	Extended along London Road to Chantry Park for the Royal Agricultural Show.
6/12/36	Return moved to Electric House to allow for cross town link services. Ranelagh Road short working probably became **Service 7A**.
31/10/38	Single loop along Dickens and Hadleigh Roads opened. This now became **Service 7A** and Ranelagh Road short working discontinued.
9/12/51	**Service 7** discontinued. **Service 7A** continued.
??/7/56	Last day of **7A**. Replaced by motorbus.

Looking back along Hadleigh Road, pre-war all Ransomes 62 is about to re-join London Road destined for Bourne Bridge on Service 1, on this occasion having completed the single line short working loop (7A) via Dickens Avenue. The Ipswich British Road Services depot was to the rear, now the site of a Sainsbury's store. Jack's transport drivers' café and accommodation was therefore ideally placed; the establishment still exists, but with a different clientele.
(H. Luff/Online Transport Archive)

SERVICE 7

The single Ransomes delivered in 1940, which was fitted with a Massey body and numbered 86, is about to begin the move around the terminal loop in London Road whilst on an enthusiasts' tour. This vehicle was the last Ransomes trolleybus to enter service in the United Kingdom; there were suggestions that it was intended to be a demonstrator for the South African market but perhaps prevented by the Second World War; no verifying evidence has been found to substantiate the claim. (A. Gordon collection)

A deserted London Road, apart from a lorry and cyclist, provide the backdrop for this rear view of Massey bodied Ransomes 76 ready to return to the town centre, after completing the turn previously referred to. This service was extended from Ranelagh Road in 1934 to provide public transport to the Royal Show held on the Chantry Estate. (A. Gordon collection)

A coloured close-up view of 76 seen above, with the current Chantry Park to the left. Note the rear bumper, and combined direction indicator and brake light.
(G. Morant/
The Transport Library)

SERVICE 8/8A

8 TOWN CENTRE – BRAMFORD ROAD – ADAIR ROAD
8A TOWN CENTRE – BRAMFORD ROAD BRIDGE (KINGSTON ROAD) (SHORT WORKING)
The majority of Service 8 return journeys were to the Station as Service X

27/7/26	Tram service to railway bridge replaced by trolleybus. Extended under low railway bridge to Adair Road necessitating the use of single deck vehicles. Departure/return Cornhill.
??/??/49	Return moved from Cornhill to Electric House (Lloyds Avenue).
14/5/50	Short working created on town side of railway bridge at the junction with Kingston Road. Allowed the use of double deck vehicles up to the railway bridge as **Service 8A**.
5/9/53	**Service 8.** Replaced by motorbus.
22/5/54	**Service 8A.** Replaced by motorbus.

In this busy August 1950 scene in the Cornhill, Ransomes 40 has arrived from Bourne Bridge or Station, and waits on the Adair Road stand under the overhead wiring out of Princes Street on the right. This photograph was taken after the introduction of a westbound one-way system along Carr, Tavern and Westgate Streets in 1949. When new, the vehicle had an open veranda next to the driver's half cab for one man "pay as you enter" operation, but was subsequently rebuilt to full front format with the entrance boarded up. A fairly new post war Standard 8 saloon completes the picture. (C. Carter)

At the same location, and with the Lloyds building as the backdrop, Ransomes 44 waits while passengers alight under the supervision of the conductor dressed in summer lightweight jacket. The nearest little boy appears to be shouldering a box camera, and the painted passenger queuing corridor can just be discerned on the pavement. Two double deck trolleybuses are in the background having arrived from Tavern Street. (J. Joyce/Online Transport Archive)

Ransomes 42 is about to begin the descent of Bramford Road on 19th July 1953, having just left the junction with Norwich Road, which is lined with a range of independent shops. These have been modified over the years, with some single storey extensions into the pavement areas. Bulwer Road leads off to the immediate right, and the shop on the corner is now a convenience store. (P. Mitchell)

SERVICE 8/8A

The next five pictures were all taken on the date of the previous picture. Ransomes 42 is seen again in Bramford Road passing the end of Kingston Road en route to the Station. The property on the right was demolished in order to create a turning circle to enable double deck vehicles to complete short workings to the town side of the low railway bridge.
(P. Mitchell)

The railway bridge that necessitated the use of single deck vehicles is illustrated here, which carried track to the Felixstowe and East Suffolk lines. Ransomes 41 is seen on the town side of the bridge, beyond which trams never ventured. The maximum headroom of 14' 3" was in the centre of the arch, and the warning notice above indicates "Danger Live Wires. Do Not Touch". This original bridge has now been replaced with a single span steel structure.
(P. Mitchell)

SERVICE 8/8A

A view from the country side of the bridge as Ransomes 42 emerges. The warning notice is repeated, and in the distance adjacent to Kingston Road is the turning circle created in 1950 to enable double deck vehicles to complete peak hour short workings (Service 8A); the circle still exists. Note the British Railway advertisement for local runabout tickets. (P. Mitchell)

Having passed under the bridge, Ransomes 41 moves along Bramford Road past the end of Wallace Road. The shop on the corner is now a hair boutique. Note the bridge warning sign. (P. Mitchell)

SERVICE 8/8A

Ransomes 43 travels along Bramford Road on route to the Station. (P. Mitchell)

Ransomes 44 is seen again turning out of Bramford Road into the Adair Road terminus with the destination already changed for the return to the Station. This vehicle was presented to the British Transport Collection in Clapham in 1955, and subsequently to the Science Museum in 1968. It was in their storage facility in Wroughton near Swindon, but is being transferred to the Ipswich Transport Museum. Note the concrete telephone box on the right.
(W. J. Haynes)

SERVICE 8/8A

A rear view of Ransomes 42 taking position ready to negotiate the terminal wiring at the wide junction of Adair and Bramford Roads. The high floor line of these 1930 vehicles necessitated the stepped entrance, and the fitting of a substantial lifeguard between the front and rear wheels. On this occasion, 42 is destined to cross town, and onwards on a linked service to Bourne Bridge as Service 1.
(S. Lockwood collection)

With "The Waveney" hotel in the background, Ransomes 43 has completed the turn ready for the return to the Station. Note the absence of the roof advertising boards, and the bulb horn on the left. The hotel site is now occupied by an apartment block.
(H. Luff/Online Transport Archive)

SERVICE 8/8A

42 has completed the turn round and waits before departing to the Station as Service X on this occasion. (H. Luff/ Online Transport Archive)

SERVICE X
TOWN CENTRE – PRINCES STREET – RAILWAY STATION

2/9/23   Initial pilot scheme to consider the use of trolleybuses to replace trams. Departure/return Cornhill.

??/??/49   Departure moved to Lloyds Avenue. Some incoming easterly and westerly services departed from Cornhill pior to the one way system being introduced, and the former there after.

??/7/56   Last day. Replaced by motorbus. Special, peak and depot workings continued until 4/62.

Many of the town's services left Cornhill to make the journey to the Station displaying Service X

The short length of Lloyds Avenue connected the two central hubs of Electric House and Cornhill, and was wired for the introduction of the one-way system along Carr, Tavern and Westgate Streets in 1949. It allowed vehicles from Crown Street and Electric House direct access to Princes and Queen Streets to the south of Cornhill. Ransomes 44 waits on stand ready to depart to the Station. Note the queueing corridor painted on the pavement.
(J. Joyce/Online Transport Archive)

SERVICE X

Massey bodied Ransomes 74 waits in Lloyds Avenue, outside the offices of Shell Mex and BP, before leaving for the Station. 74 has completed one of the double deck inward services to Electric House, and will continue on as Service X to the Station.
(R. Marshall/The Bus Archive)

At the same location is Park Royal bodied AEC Regent 4, one of the first six motorbuses delivered in 1950 that signalled the start of the gradual conversion of the trolleybus system in the town. To the rear are two later similar vehicles, and an absence of trolleybuses, although overhead wiring is still in place.
(Online Transport Archive)

This July 1951 photograph depicts Massey bodied Ransomes 69 waiting in Cornhill before moving onward to the Station. This is another example of an inward bound vehicle continuing on to this destination as 69 has arrived from one of the eastern services. The Burton's building is immediately behind next to the premises of shoe retailer Freeman, Hardy and Willis; the latter's name originates from three of the original employees. The name was no more after 1996, with a number of branches sold to Stead and Simpson. Note another example of a painted queueing corridor. (J. C. Gillham)

Ransomes 41 passes under the Lloyd Avenue arch en route to the Station on 19th July 1953, although the destination display continues to show the outward service to Adair Road. Further back along Lloyds Avenue, an Eastern Counties Bristol single decker is on a local town service, as naval ratings occupy the pavement. (P. Mitchell)

SERVICE X

In April 1956 Karrier W 100 also passes under the Lloyds Avenue arch to enter into the Cornhill, and then onwards along Princes Street to the Station. The side advertisement is for the long-established Ipswich ironmonger Martin and Newby, where virtually any item of hardware could be purchased. (A. Gordon collection)

Ransomes 42 descends Princes Street on 19th July 1953, with the Barclays Bank building in the distance. The printer's premises on the left looks as though it has been abandoned, and is now part of the Wolsey House site.
(P. Mitchell)

On the same day as the previous picture, 42 is seen again in Princes Street about to cross the railway and river bridges before turning into Burrell Road, and the Station. Commercial Road is in the right foreground, and the whole area has seen significant change, with Commercial Road now one-way Commercial Way, with the buildings in the background having been swept away to be replaced by a fire station, post office sorting facility and retail outlets. A Wolseley saloon brings up the rear. (P. Mitchell)

With a malthouse on the skyline, Karrier 114 crosses the bridge over the River Orwell before turning into Burrell Road and the terminus. On the right is the British Road Services Parcel Depot; all that can be seen back along Princes Street has been swept away to be replaced by buildings indicated in the last caption. (P. Mitchell)

Looking in the opposite direction, Ransomes 43 crosses the bridge over the River Orwell on a return to Adair Road. The appearance of the vehicle is somewhat improved due to the absence of advertising boards, and the bamboo boom retrieval pole can be seen secured immediately above the opening windows.
(H. Luff/Online Transport Archive)

A bicycle is kerb parked on the corner outside the Station Hotel as Ransomes 42 turns out of Princes Street into Burrell Road ready to turn outside the station forecourt; the destination blind has alreadybeen changed ready for the return to Adair Road. The malt house building on the right was a night club, but has now been converted into office accommodation. (D. A. Jones/East Anglia Transport Museum)

At the same location, Massey bodied Ransomes 76 has just crossed the bridge over the River Orwell, with Princes Street stretching back towards the town centre. At least three cyclists appear to be taking liquid refreshment in the Station Hotel.
(R. Morant/The Transport Library)

Sunbeam 126 completes the turn back outside the station forecourt, but by the time this photograph was taken in April 1961 the overhead wiring along Burrell Road in the background had been removed. Wiring along this road relates back to tramway days when a special service was provided from the station to the landing stage on the River Orwell to enable passengers to embark on one of the three river steamers operated by the London and North Eastern Railway, having been initiated earlier by the Great Eastern Railway. When trolleybuses were introduced, wiring was installed to provide an electrical supply to Stoke Bridge. On the left is a General Post Office (GPO) Karrier Gamecock linesmen's mobile workshop.
(D. Pearson)

On a warm day with windscreens open, Ransomes 41 completes the Station turn to move towards the waiting passengers. The overhead wiring joining the turning circle out of Burrell Road to the rear, which leads down to Stoke Bridge, was never used other than for emergency workings and enthusiasts' specials. The overhead was tied off at Stoke Bridge, so there was no physical connection, although the wiring provided an electrical supply between the two locations. (D. A. Jones/East Anglia Transport Museum)

Three trolleybuses wait in front of the station forecourt with 41 seen again destined for Adair Road on Service 8; all three are under the nearside wiring, with parallel overhead providing a passing loop. In the left background, the start of the turning loop can be seen, with wiring that continued into Burrell Road. For an unidentified period, there was parallel wiring along the left hand side of the road up to the beginning of the turning loop. (A. Gordon collection)

Ransomes 43, minus advertising boards, waits on stand before returning to Adair Road on 19th July 1953. Note the style of light fittings mounted on the traction standards. The substantial passenger shelter on the right no longer exists.
(P. Mitchell)

Karrier W 92 waits on the Station stand before returning to the Cornhill, and onwards to Whitton on Service 9.
(A. Gordon collection)

SERVICE X

Park Royal bodied AEC Regent motorbus 1, destined for the White House Estate, is from the initial batch of diesel vehicles delivered in 1950, which broke the trolleybus monopoly of municipal public transport in the town. In front, Ransomes 43, without advertising boards, waits to leave for Adair Road in August 1950; note how each boom base is mounted one above the other. (C. Carter)

Sunbeam 118 leaves the Station for an outward journey to Witton on Service 9. This is another example of one of the town's double deck services having made a trip from Cornhill to the Station on Service X. (A. Belton)

SERVICE 11
TOWN CENTRE – WOODBRIDGE ROAD – SIDEGATE LANE

10/4/47   Service opened.
Short working at Colchester Road traffic island; removed circa 1957.
Departure/return Electric House.

1/6/59   Regular service replaced by motorbus other than peak and school specials.

?/10/60   Completely replaced by motorbus.

Karrier 115, returning from Sidegate Lane in May 1962, has entered Tower Street, the eastern side of the Electric House terminus, and will shortly reach the service stand outside the Tower Ramparts school. A Ford Consul stands in front of the Egerton car showrooms, now a Yates pub and restaurant. (A. Gordon collection)

SERVICE 11

Having reached the north side of Electric House, Karrier W 102 waits under the nearside overhead wiring on the Sidegate Lane stand in June 1951. Beyond what is possibly a Morris 14 in the car park, a double deck Ransomes can be seen; note the queuing corridor for the Felixstowe Road service painted on the pavement.
(R. Marshall/The Bus Archive)

Sunbeam 118 leaves the north side of the Electric House, with what appears to be a good level of lower deck passengers. (Author's collection)

SERVICE 11

Sunbeam 112 has just left St Margaret's Street, and entered Woodbridge Road on an outward journey. The garage and Territorial Army building next to 112 have since been demolished to provide a car park.

(S. N. J. White)

Karrier 114 returns to Electric House along Woodbridge Road, having just crossed the bridge over the railway line to Felixstowe adjacent to the Double Diamond advertisement in the background. Note how the three twin line hangers suspended from the cantilevered bracket arm to the rear have been used to deal with the curve in the overhead wiring to match that of the road.

(P. Mitchell)

SERVICE 11

On a return from Sidegate Lane on 16th May 1959, Sunbeam 123 moves along Woodbridge Road, with the junction into the former in the background. This junction also featured in a BICC overhead equipment catalogue. (P. Mitchell)

Karrier W 97 has just passed under a section insulator/feeder having crossed Colchester Road when travelling along Sidegate Lane, where a traffic island provided a short working facility; this was subsequently removed. The unit at the top of the parallel posts is a wartime air raid siren. (A. Valentine/Ipswich Transport Museum)

Sidegate Lane stretches back into the far distance towards the terminus as Karrier 111 rounds the bend, and will shortly cross Colchester Road before continuing onwards to the junction with Woodbridge Road in May 1959.
(P. Mitchell)

Whilst on an enthusiasts' special, the lone 1940 Massey bodied Ransomes 86 has completed the Sidegate Lane turn back slightly to the rear, and has paused for a photograph to be taken. In the background are the post-war prefabricated bungalows, commonly referred to as "pre-fabs", built in 1946 in an effort to deal with the immediate post war housing shortage. They are still occupied today.
(Author's collection)

SERVICE 11

At the destination of Service 11 amongst local authority housing stock, a specially constructed turning circle was provided in which Karrier W 104 stands waiting to return to Electric House on 16th April 1955. The circle still exists, but now tends to be used for local residents' car parking. (P. Mitchell)

This second view of the terminus depicts Weymann bodied Karrier W 87 waiting to return to the town centre. (S. Lockwood collection)

SERVICE O
CIRCULARS/COLCHESTER ROAD
Clockwise circular outwards via Woodbridge Road
Anti-clockwise circular outward via Felixstowe Road

6/12/36 Wiring was erected along Woodbridge, Rushmere, Colchester, Heath, Bixley Roads and along Felixstowe Road to join existing wiring at Kings Way. A regular turnback at the junction of Rushmere Road and Colchester Road received no service number.
Departure/return Electric House

9/12/51 Regular circular services discontinued other than peak, school and workmen specials.

30/5/59 Last day. Colchester Road and circular services replaced by motorbus.

A turn back towards town was provided on the clockwise circuit at the junction of Rushmere and Colchester Roads. Although destination blinds listed Colchester Road as a destination, no service number was ever allocated. Sunbeam 123 turns into Tower Street with the destination blind already changed for the un-numbered service. (Author's collection)

Karrier W 93 waits on stand outside the Tower Ramparts school, with the destination depicting an outward anti-clockwise circular journey along Felixstowe Road, and a return via Woodbridge Road.

(R. Marshall/The Bus Archive)

Pre-war Ransomes vehicles are illustrated here outside the Tower Ramparts school. In the foreground the unique Massey bodied 86 waits on stand before departing on the Colchester Road service, whilst under the passing loop, Massey bodied 83 departs on Service 6B to Gainsborough. The car park provides a good selection of period vehicles.

(H. N. James/Ipswich Transport Museum)

86 is seen again moving along the north side of Electric House (Crown Street) on an outward circular trip, again via Felixstowe Road. In the background is the extensive Egerton garage and the Cricketers Hotel.

(R. Marshall/The Bus Archive)

This poor image has been included to illustrate the overall grey livery that was applied to vehicles delivered immediately after the war. Karrier W 102 has left Fore Street, and has begun to climb Fore Hamlet on an outward clockwise circular. Note the narrowness of the roadway, which has already been widened to the rear of the photographer; property to the right is in the process of being demolished to continue the process.

(Author's collection)

SERVICE O

Karrier 114 moves along Rushmere Road on 16th May 1959 returning to Electric House, having just negotiated the Colchester Road traffic island in the background. Note the Austin car on the left carrying registration number BRT 1 (Suffolk County Council 1936).
(P. Mitchell)

Karrier W 91 waits at the terminal stand of the Colchester Road service in Rushmere Road on 8th June 1957. 91 has turned back to the town centre around the traffic island in the background, with overhead wiring off to the right along Colchester Road leading towards Woodbridge Road, which was used by the circular services.
(P. Mitchell)

This rear view of Karrier W 101, at the same location, was taken looking in the opposite direction to the previous image. On leaving for Electric House, 101 will pass under a section insulator/feeder; these were inserted every half mile to ensure that an electrical failure in one section did not affect those either side. It was usually where electrical power was fed into the overhead from a local substation, as seen in this view. To help drivers identify where they should "coast" (take no power) under the section insulator, two white bands were painted on the supporting traction standard.
(A. Valentine/ Ipswich Transport Museum)

On 16th June 1962, Karrier W 111 waits at the St Augustine's stand before making a return to the town centre on a clockwise circuit along Felixstowe Road.
(P. Mitchell)

SERVICE O

At the same location and date as the previous picture, AEC Regent 1 from the original motorbus delivery of 1950, has arrived from Bixley Road, and awaits departure to Electric House on the trolleybus service. (P. Mitchell)

DEPOTS

Constantine Road
This depot was built for the opening of the tramway system in 1903 together with power station, office block and refuse destructor. The trolleybus entrance was to the rear with vehicles travelling along Portman's Walk, now Sir Alf Ramsay Way, to exit from the front of the building into Constantine Road. The depot is still used by the current Ipswich fleet.

Ransomes 43 approaches the depot whilst on an enthusiasts' special. Overhead wiring from a depot exit road leads in from the right. The area beyond the fencing belongs to Ipswich Town Football Club, and the then Portman's Walk stretches back to Portman Road. (D. A. Jones/East Anglia Transport Museum)

DEPOTS

Karrier 114 is parked, with booms down, on the depot exit forecourt; overhead wiring along Portman's Walk leading to the rear entrance can be seen on the right. (Author's collection)

In a similar location on 19th July 1953, Ransomes 38 has destination blinds displaying one of the circular services, and in the side destination, the short working to Tyler Street Service 1A. (P. Mitchell)

DEPOTS

Inside the depot looking out towards Constantine Road with Sunbeam 126 and Karrier W 108; the former is awaiting departure on an enthusiasts' tour. Note the evidence of tram track, the substantial cycle rack, and the maximum use of advertising space on the rear of the vehicles. (D. Pearson)

With evidence of tram track bottom left, all Ransomes 56 leads the middle road, with an unidentified Sunbeam on the left. (D. A. Jones/East Anglia Transport Museum)

DEPOTS

Priory Heath

The Priory Heath depot began to be used from December 1936, but was opened officially as a trolleybus depot and workshop in March 1937. Access was through the front from Cobham Road, and egress at the rear into Wright Road. The depot was used by motorbuses for a while before closure, and is now the refurbished site of the highly recommended Ipswich Transport Museum.

Karrier 112 leaves Cobham Road to begin the turn into the depot, having completed a short working to Kings Way.
(A. Belton)

The front elevation of the depot is illustrated here, with Sunbeam 115 about to enter in June 1961; on the left a vehicle can be seen in the paint shop. 115 has left the Service 4 at Kings Way, a short distance away, as indicated by the destination display; passengers were allowed to travel to this point before vehicles entered the depot.
(D. Pearson)

A view inside the depot taken in October 1961 looking towards the exit at the rear of the building, with Karrier 113 taking centre stage.
(J. C. Gillham)

With the sunlight shining through the front entrance, Ransomes 65 leads a line of parked vehicles.
(D. A. Jones/East Anglia Transport Museum)

DEPOTS

At the rear of the depot, Karrier W 101 is positioned under one of the exit overhead lines leading into Wright Road. Examples of this Park Royal bodied vehicle were purchased by Derby, Nottingham, Maidstone, Walsall, South Shields and Reading amongst others, on both Sunbeam and Karrier branded chassis. (D. Pearson)

Inside the body shop, a Massey bodied Ransomes is undergoing a major refurbishment, particularly in the offside cab area. Note the mobile tower to enable work to be carried out on the upper areas.
(D. A. Jones/East Anglia Transport Museum)

Having left the rear of the depot, and travelled the short distance along Wright Road, Karrier 113 turns into Cobham Road leading up to the Kings Way junction to join Felixstowe Road. Beyond the boundary on the opposite side of the road is the railway line from Ipswich to Felixstowe town and port facility.

(A. Gordon collection)

Looking along Cobham Road towards Kings Way and Felixstowe Road, Karrier 112 has just left Wright Road as it leaves the depot, and is about to travel the length of Lindbergh Road to take up service at Priory Heath.

(A. Valentine/Ipswich Transport Museum)

DEPOTS

With the overhead wiring for Priory Heath depot in the distance, Karrier 114 moves along Cobham Road towards the Kings Way/Felixstowe Road junction. To the left is the railway cutting for the Felixstowe line. (P. Mitchell)

On leaving the depot, Karrier 111 makes the extremely tight turn out of Cobham Road into Felixstowe Road, and onto the bridge incline over the railway line to Felixstowe. In the background, an Eastern Counties Bristol Lodekka leaves Kings Way; this three-way road junction was the original terminus for Service 4 before the extension to St Augustine's. The gentleman on the left looking skyward seems to have identified that the driver of 111 has stopped under an insulated "dead section" of the overhead turnout, and therefore unable to move forward. One solution would be to allow the vehicle to roll back slightly into Cobham Road thereby clearing the dead section.
(A. Gordon collection)

THE AFTER LIFE

After the pre-war single deck vehicles were withdrawn, many were snapped up by market gardeners, farmers and builders to provide additional storage or office accommodation; this picture provides an example of the former. (A. Valentine/Ipswich Transport Museum)

After withdrawal in April 1962, Karrier W 105 was used as an exhibition vehicle, and is seen here parked outside the Old Town Hall in the Cornhill, where it is being used to publicise Civil Defence. The Golden Lion Hotel in the background has occupied the site for around 500 years. (A. Valentine/Ipswich Transport Museum)

THE AFTER LIFE

Next, 105 was converted into a canteen, which was located on the Electric House car park, with the Egerton garage in the background. It was provided with an electrical supply and curtains; the waste bins, and a milk bottle carrier under the platform complete the picture.
(C. Carter)

There are static displays at the Museum, which include 1950 Sunbeam 126 (returned from Walsall), one of the original 1923 Railless vehicles (2) which opened the system, and 1933 Ransomes 46 awaiting major refurbishment. On the same day as in the next picture, Railless 2 was taken to the East Anglia Transport Museum, and exhibited as a static display. The restoration of these vehicles is another example of the dedicated work carried out by the Ipswich Transport Museum volunteer staff.
(S. Ray)

THE AFTER LIFE

After serving time as a mobile canteen, 105 has been fully re-furbished to an operational condition by the voluntary museum staff, and was operated around the East Anglia Transport Museum circuit at Carlton Colville, Suffolk, as seen in this picture. Note the green wheels, which were standard up to 1958, after which red was specified as indicated on Ipswich's AEC Regent 1 in the background; 105 was the first trolleybus to receive red wheels. The destination blind has been set for the short working Service 9A to Norwich Road Bridge.
(S. Ray)

THE AFTER LIFE

Sunbeams 119 to 126 were sold to Walsall Corporation in February 1962. Apart from one accident withdrawal, they were subsequently transferred to the West Midlands Passenger Transport Executive in 1969, and withdrawn in 1970.

Walsall 344 (Ipswich 123) is seen here at the rear of the ABC Cinema in Townsend Street, which was the loading point for Service 29 to Wolverhampton, jointly operated by the two municipalities. To the rear is one of the ex-Hastings Sunbeams purchased by Walsall in 1959. The overall blue Walsall livery was in stark contrast to Ipswich's green, cream and burnished aluminium. The destination aperture provided a challenge for the destination blind maker, which was solved by printing "Wolverhampton" diagonally. (Author's collection)

THE AFTER LIFE

Walsall 353 (Ipswich 121) makes the tight turn at the end of St Paul's Street to enter the Central Bus Station before continuing on Service 30 to Bloxwich. The St Paul's church is in the immediate background, although the area in front has now been pedestrianised.
(Author's collection)

At the Central Bus Station in St Pauls Street, Walsall 354 (Ipswich 122) waits on stand before departing on the circular Service 33 via the Dudley Fields Estate. This vehicle was involved in a serious accident when it overturned whilst operating on Service 29 (Walsall to Wolverhampton) on 26th July 1965, resulting in one fatality. Damage to the vehicle was so severe it never re-entered service.
(Author's collection)

On 3rd October 1970, the last day of operation of the Walsall system, Sunbeam 353 (Ipswich 121) turns into the Bloxwich terminus with an assortment of period cars in view. (P. Thomas)

THE AFTER LIFE

This photograph is somewhat confusing as Walsall 347 (Ipswich 126) is displaying its home town as the destination, when in fact it is leaving the town towards Willenhall. This is confirmed by the Reedswood, also known as Walsall, Power Station in the background, which has since been demolished. The scene is Wolverhampton Road West just beyond the western side of the current M6, with 347 being followed by a Wolseley 15/60 in October 1965. (P. Thomas)

The block of flats gives this picture an Eastern European feel as Sunbeam 351 (Ipswich 119) travels back to its home town past the gates of Bentley Cemetery in Wolverhampton Road West on the same date as the previous picture. 351 is about to pass under a section insulator/electrical feeder, and be overtaken by a Wolseley 1500, with a Hillman Imp facing in the opposite direction.
(P. Thomas)

On the joint service to Wolverhampton, Sunbeam 352 (Ipswich 120) leaves Wolverhampton Road, now known as Somerford Place, as it passes the Portobello School in Willenhall, and is about to enter High Street Portobello, now called Willenhall Road, in October 1965. (P. Thomas)

THE AFTER LIFE

The Wolverhampton terminus of the joint Service 29 from Walsall was in St James's Square. Here we see Walsall 346 (Ipswich 125) waiting on stand before returning to its home town via Willenhall, with a Wolverhampton Roe re-bodied Sunbeam W to the rear. (P. Thomas)

On 26th June 1965 Sunbeam 354 (Ipswich 122) was blown over as a result of a heavy gust of wind, resulting in one pedestrian fatality, and thirteen injured passengers. After recovery it was not considered worth repairing, and was duly scrapped. These two photographs show the extent of the damage after 354 had been recovered. (Both E. Challoner collection)

THE END OF AN ERA

Once the trolleybus operations had ceased the final chapter was the removal of the above ground infrastructure. Traction standards and overhead wiring had been a feature of the Ipswich street scene since 1903, and the linesmen who had conscientiously maintained the overhead wiring were now tasked with its gradual removal, knowing that when completed, their jobs would no longer exist. The next five images show the linesmen at work on this final task. Included in three of the images is the Ransomes battery tower wagon DX 3578, which had helped with the original installation of overhead wiring in the 1920s'. (All images A. Valentine/Ipswich Transport Museum)

THE END OF AN ERA

THE END OF AN ERA

FLEET LIST

Fleet No	Registration No	Chassis	Body	Seating	In Service
1-3 (A)	DX3870/88/06	Railless	Short	B30F	1923
4	DX4648	Ransomes	Ransomes	B30F	1924
5	DX5217	Tilling Stevens	Ransomes	B30F	1925
6 (B)	DX5409	Ransomes	Ransomes	B30F	1926
6-20 (C/D)	DX5622/08-21	Ransomes	Ransomes	B30D	1926
21-35 (E/F)	DX5626/23-25/28/29/27/30-32/34/33/35-37	Garrett	Strachan & Brown	B30D	1926
36-41 (G)	DX6014/7620/33/51/68/83	Ransomes	Ransomes	B34D (36) / B30D (37-40) / B30D (41)	1928 / 1928 / 1929
42-44 (H)	DX8869-71	Ransomes	Ransomes	B30D	1930
45	DX9610	Garrett	Garrett	B31C	1931
46-49 (I)	PV817-820	Ransomes	Ransomes	H24/24R	1933
50-59	PV1253-56/1350-55	Ransomes	Ransomes	H24/24R	1934
60-67	PV2727-34	Ransomes	Ransomes	H24/24R	1936
68-79	PV4061-66/4540-45	Ransomes	Massey	H24/24R	1937/38
80-85	PV4788-93	Ransomes	Massey	H24/24R	1938
86	PV6426	Ransomes	Massey	H24/24R	1940
87-90	PV6875-78	Karrier W	Weymann	H30/26R	1944
91-102	PV6891-96/6950-55	Karrier W	Park Royal	H30/26R	1945
103-108 (J)	PV8268-73	Karrier W	Park Royal	H30/26R	1948
109-114	PV8866-71	Karrier F4	Park Royal	H30/26R	1949
115-126 (K)	ADX185-96	Sunbeam F4	Park Royal	H30/26R	1950

A	2 is a restored static exhibit at the Ipswich Transport Museum.
B	Ransomes demonstrator; returned to manufacturer 4/26.
C	9 is in storage at the Ipswich Transport Museum.
D	16 chassis an exhibit at the Ipswich Transport Museum.
E	26 under restoration at the Long Shop Museum, Leiston.
F	29 chassis an exhibit at the Long Shop Museum, Leiston.
G	36 was a Ransomes demonstrator.
H	44 being transferred from Science Museum storage to Ipswich Transport Museum.
I	46 is a static display at the Ipswich Transport Museum awaiting restoration.
J	105 converted into a mobile canteen; now an operational exhibit at the Ipswich Transport Museum.
K	119 – 126 sold to Walsall Corporation in 1962. 126 is an exhibit at the Ipswich Transport. Walsall fleet numbers 351–354/344–347.

Notes

W	Wartime Ministry utility specification.
B30F	Single deck vehicle with 30 seats and a front entrance/exit.
B30D	Single deck vehicle with 30 seats and separate entrance and exit.
B30C	Single deck vehicle with 30 seats and a central entrance/exit.
H24/24R	Double deck vehicle with 24 seats on both decks and a rear entrance/exit.
H30/26R	Double deck vehicle with 30 seats on lower deck and 26 upper with a rear entrance/exit.